Losing Everything

A Family's Journey with Alzheimer's Disease

By S. P. Murray

Strategic Book Publishing and Rights Co.

Strategic Book Publishing and Rights Co., LLC
USA | Singapore

For information about special discounts for bulk purchases, please
contact Strategic Book Publishing and Rights Co. Special Sales, at
bookorder@sbpra.net.

ISBN: 978-1-946540-08-9

Book Design: Suzanne Kelly

DEDICATION

This book is dedicated to my mom, who was once a beautiful and giving person.

Mom, you lived your life the best way you knew how and lost who you are far too young because of this horrible disease.

I would also like to dedicate this book to all the people caring for Alzheimer's patients. This includes all the distraught spouses, children, family members, and total strangers caring for people who lack any inkling of who they are and are incapable of any normal response to what goes on around them. May your journey, and mine, improve someday soon, and may we all be rewarded with health and long life. My wish for you is the same as for myself: that we be given strength and steadfast support by the unseen and all-knowing God of heaven.

Caring for those with this disease requires dedication, and I applaud all of you who stand firm offering backbreaking and nerve-racking work in an insurmountable situation that can only worsen with time. May we be blessed, for each day that comes to us we keep pouring goodwill down a black hole that in time will only get deeper, with no end in sight.

Despite our courage and all the strength we can muster, we know that with each passing moment the one for whom we care will keep slipping further and further into that dark place named Alzheimer's.

ACKNOWLEDGMENTS

A heartfelt and sincere thank-you to my late Aunt Deloris for caring for Mom in the early stages of her disease, for your generous kindness and patience with her and for giving her a loving home for seven months, for putting up with her many mood swings and bad habits. Your journey in this life was way too short—you passed away too soon, but I am positive that God's grace was always with you, and I hope you find peace in your forever rest.

To my older sister, Amy, who cared for Mom for a year and struggled each day to understand "why," for doing your best and in the process almost losing the most precious gift anyone can have: life. May your heath continue to improve; I hope one day you can be restored to the "you" you used to be.

To my younger sister, Sally, thank you for not giving up on Mom and for bearing the brunt of her rage for so many years.

To Annie, a/k/a Ms. Muffin, your care and support for Mom is something I can never repay. From the bottom of my heart, I thank you for always being there for her and for being so kind and thoughtful in your daily challenges with her. Your dedication to her is priceless.

To Cindy, my cousin, the positive little engine that always can. Your support and assistance with Mom is always appreciated. Nothing is ever too hard for you, and you never say no when it comes to being there for her.

To my brother, Nick, who took my scribbles from hundreds of handwritten pages I wrote over the past few years and turned them into the typewritten word. Thanks for your time and effort in bringing this sad story to life!

To my friend Dr. Benway, for taking the time to read the first draft of Mom's story and giving me helpful comments and tips, and encouraging me to continue to document our struggles. It is truly appreciated.

To my friend and colleague Joakim, for agreeing to read the second draft of the book, and for being brutally honest by telling me I should tell the entire story no matter what. I thank you for your honesty and encouragement.

To author David Holmberg, who gave me constructive criticism and editorial assistance.

And last but certainly not least, to my dear, sweet husband, Stephen, who has steadfastly stood by me as I supported Mom emotionally and financially. My heart belongs to you!

CONTENTS

INTRODUCTION}

I began a journal of Mom's decline because I wanted to document my feelings and remember what Mom used to be before her decline into what I describe as madness. My journal is sad, frustrating, at times depressing, and courageous—but most of all it's loving, because it comes from a desire to understand and protect Mom.

The disease that afflicts Mom is Alzheimer's. This condition is like no other in its capacity to disrupt and irrevocably upend an individual's life—in this case my mother's good and productive life. In its attack mode, this devastating illness also profoundly affects the victim's loved ones. Mom's illness has cast such a long, dark shadow on my life that at times I can't clearly remember the life I had prior to her disease. Mom's illness seemed like it came storming in; it arrived without our knowledge and has slowly but surely taken over every aspect of our daily existence.

The striking theme of this book is my difficulty in adjusting to the reality of Mom's condition. I've referred to her as "the one I lost." I detail how alone I feel in my struggle to understand, because I am at a loss to comprehend how we have come to this point in life.

I grieve on a daily basis because I have lost Mom. However, my grief does not go away because her body is still alive. Yet she is lost because she does not know who we are. In the pages that follow, I wonder who this stranger is that has emerged. I don't know this person and have no idea what to believe about her anymore. I've tried for years to understand this disease and have failed miserably, because the more I learn about Alzheimer's, the less I understand. This disease hijacked everything I thought I knew about Mom.

I worry that one day I too may get this terrible disease. I worry about what will happen to Mom if I die before she does. God forbid! Who else would want to bear the burden of caring for her financially?

There are many other themes and concerns in this tragic story: My decision to medicate Mom, which I came to with reluctance and apprehension; the nature of her deterioration, which is erratic, progressive, and exhausting; the necessity for constant alertness and the daily assaults of this disease; my devotion and duty to Mom; and, hopefully, my abiding patience even though I feel besieged.

And beyond my devotion to her, I can't refrain from asking the inevitable question that so many dedicated caregivers ask: "Is it wrong to want my life back?"

The answer, I believe, is no, just as the answer is obviously yes to another question: "Is Alzheimer's a scourge to be endured and, unfortunately, accepted until the day a cure is found, if such a day ever comes?"

LACK OF CELEBRATION

Today is February 20, 2014. It's Mom's seventy-fourth birthday. Today should have been a day of celebration with dinner, cake, and guests, but it is not. My beautiful mom had no idea it was her birthday. She had no clue what year, month, day, or even hour it was. Even if I told her what day it was, she would forget in seconds.

Annie and Cindy prepared a small dinner and baked a cake. Cindy enlarged and framed two photos of Mom dating back forty-plus years. They are now hanging on the wall in the dining room. I asked Mom, "Who is in the picture?" At first she said it was her, but a few minutes later, she told me how lovely I look in the picture. "Are you sure it's me in the photo?" She replied that she is forgetting a lot these days and was unsure who was in the picture.

Watching Mom now fills me with sorrow. I had hoped when she joined the senior citizen ranks that, with the help of her children, life would become kinder to her. It is now apparent that hope will never be fulfilled. Rather, she is concluding this life at the end of a very short stick.

How can one reconcile something with such horrific consequences? Her entire life was terrible, and now this repugnant disease seems to have simply taken everything away from her. When she finally leaves this life, she will do so knowing absolutely nothing, including who she is.

It would be easier if I saw a stranger when I look at her, but I don't. I see the person who used to be Mom but in reality no longer is Mom. Now when I look in her eyes, I don't even see her ghost. Her eyes are dead. There is no longer any spark. It is so bad now that I no longer call her "Mother" because it seems to annoy her. According to her, I cannot be her daughter because

I am too old. Whatever recording is playing in her brain, it does not include a daughter my age. If, as she claims, she is in her twenties or thirties, then her children are a lot younger than I am. It is the most difficult thing for a child not to be recognized by the only parent she has ever known and loved.

In the summer of 2013, the doctor said it would be better to address her by her name, so I began calling her B, short for Barbara.

At times she is in a playful mood, but most of the time she is angry or frustrated. I suppose you would be too if you walked around knowing you had lost something, but you had no idea exactly what you had lost. Maybe that is the worst part of the disease: It makes you forget but curses you with the awareness that you forgot something.

She does not like us touching her now. There was a time when she could not have enough hugs and kisses, but those days are long gone. If we touch her, she shrinks away from us. Once in a while, if she is in a particularly unpleasant mood and we try to hug or touch her, she will advance toward us in a threatening manner, like an animal responding to a threat. When this occurs, we've learned to back away without any sudden movements to avoid exacerbating the situation even more. One minute later, the entire thing is forgotten and the incident is gone from her mind.

A few weeks ago, I told my husband that Mom is dead. She's certainly not around any longer, not the person I used to call Mom. She somehow vanished without much warning. It seemed as though, overnight, someone or something came, scooped out her brain, and took her far away. Stephen said it was not nice to say she is dead. Regretfully, I remain convinced that she *is* dead. Her heart beats, but there is no brain. Well, her brain sort of works, but not the way it is supposed to.

ALZHEIMER'S

What is Alzheimer's? I am not interested in the clinical definitions, as Google is too close at hand for that. I pose the question as a curious outsider looking in on an ongoing drama that is being played out on the stage of Mom's life. What the hell is this disease?

Here is my personal perspective. It is an unwelcome, unwanted guest that moves in without notice or fanfare. It stealthily becomes a resident deep inside the mind and slowly, but deliberately, removes the precious elements of life. Researchers believe it sets up residence fifteen to twenty years before it manifests itself. It's almost like it has to redecorate and tinker with the mechanics and engineering of the brain before showing itself for what it really is. By the time you realize what is occurring, there is nothing that can be done. The end is inevitably cruel and devastatingly efficient, and the final outcome—well, it is just a matter of time.

How can anyone defend against an adversary that is so devious and yet so thorough? Alzheimer's is the enemy that will always be the victor. We have become accustomed to someone dying physically, and then simultaneously that person's mind goes too. The curse of this disease is that it kills your mind but leaves your physical presence intact. It's a parasite that kills the most essential part of the host but allows the body to keep on living.

We know the story of Job from the Bible. Job had disaster after disaster visited upon him. In one of the chapters, he asked that the day of his birth be extracted from the calendar and discarded forever. At times I feel like Job in that whatever can go wrong does go wrong. I want Alzheimer's gone, thrown away, extracted from the calendar of time.

For the past few years, as the disease has marched on, two songs have played over and over in my head. Not a day goes by when they don't pop into my brain and I either sing or hum to myself. In the first song, "America," Paul Simon sings about being lost, empty, and aching. I feel that way too; I am really scared of the unknown, the future, the inevitable, but most of all I wonder if this awful disease has already set up residence in my own brain. Will I become a hollow shell without a past or the possibility of a future? I am afraid to be tested to see if there is a genetic probability that I carry this disease. Fear hovers over me. If I think I see something or, God forbid, I forget something, the fear overwhelms me and there is no one to shush it away.

There are tons of books written on this disease, many of which pose great questions, but none carry any answers. There are many helpful suggestions on what can be done to push this disease temporarily into the future or maybe even sidestep it altogether, but there are no guarantees.

Because of what I have witnessed, I need guarantees that I will not get this awful disease. Without this guarantee, what's left? Only fear.

The second song, "Don't Let the Sun Go Down on Me," is by Elton John. In Mom's case, she has lost everything and, indeed, the sun has gone down on her. But that still leaves us, her children. Are we going to lose everything before we have to? Will this disease make the sun go down on us in the midday hour of our lives? People begin to ail or just get tired and eventually fade into death. But this disease turns fully animated people into zombies, refusing to let them lie down and sleep. It accomplishes this years before they are finally allowed to rest.

In my childhood, I recall one woman who was a bit off-center. She recognized her daughter-in-law and made sure she told her off every day. I am not sure what was wrong with her, but I don't think she had this disease because she remembered a lot.

Now I know so many people with this disease. What has gone so wrong that so many people now suffer from this disease?

I have a friend whose father has the disease. We had a conversation recently and he told me his dad had a healthy lifestyle. He abstained from drinking, smoking, and drugs and was a vegetarian his entire life, and he still got this disease. His dad sometimes wakes up in the middle of the night screaming that someone is trying to kill him and he cannot breathe. My friend thinks his dad is actually forgetting the mechanics of breathing properly at night, and when he stops breathing, he wakes up in a panic. I cannot say if this is true. What I do know is this disease takes everything from its victims and leaves them with nothing at all!

CHILDHOOD

As I try to figure out what went wrong with Mom, I return often to my childhood. We were very poor, with little money and few friends.

Mom was a teenage mother and a single parent of four before her twenty-eighth birthday. She made up her mind that she would rather be alone than continue to be abused by our biological father. I am sure it was not easy for her to leave, but I knew then, as I know now, that she had no choice. I don't know if all the beatings she took from him contributed to her illness. I don't know if having to take care of us and not having time for herself contributed to her disease. She was not extremely sociable, and I don't know if that contributed to her lot in this life.

Mom's younger brother, two years her junior, is also sick with this disease. It baffles me how both of them could have ended up with this condition. Mom is one of twelve children, three of whom died in childhood. Out of the remaining nine, just she and her brother are afflicted with the disease. Whatever it was in their upbringing that laid the foundation for this disease to eventually flourish is unknown.

During our childhood, our grandparents took care of us while Mom worked. Mom was always very proud of our little accomplishments and did her best to encourage us. She sacrificed like a dog with little compensation, and now in her golden years, when she should have her just reward, she has no idea who she is.

How can this be fair to her and her children? As a child, I always wished for a better life. When I finally matured, I was fortunate to get that better life. I always wanted Mom to have what she had missed out on when she was young. I was trying to give that life to her when she was struck down. I know this will sound funny, but I feel cheated for her. Oh, how I wish I could have done more for her, and because this opportunity was taken away from me prematurely, I cannot help but feel cheated.

LIFE AS WE KNOW IT

Mom emigrated from the Caribbean to the United States in 1970, when we were quite young. Mom always told us she had had a difficult life. As a child, she was the babysitter for her siblings and hated it. She was looking for a way out when she found our biological father. She moved into his mother's house and her life became progressively worse.

My oldest sister, Amy, Mom's first, was born when Mom was a teenager. Mom was a child herself and her husband at the time was twenty-four. Fast-forward to today and a relationship like theirs would be a crime!

Because of her unhappy childhood and her desire to get away from her parents' home, she assumed her husband would love her. Perhaps for the first time in her life she could be happy, but, alas, she was sadly mistaken.

Her husband was verbally, emotionally, and physically abusive to her. He would beat her mercilessly. In the late 1950s and into the 1960s, smoking and drinking were considered cool and most people did it. That was the culture. Some drank and smoked more than others; our father drank and smoked more than anyone I knew. In his drunken state, Mom had the power and stature to beat him senseless, but she did not. She took what he dished out; to this day I don't know why. My father's mother was no better. She also abused my mother verbally. My grandmother would call Mom a liar and tell her how lazy and stupid she was on a daily basis. When Mom was well, she would tell stories of what had been done to her by these two people. It was simply heartbreaking. Even though we were very young, I can recall some of the fighting and beatings.

I have a vivid memory of one of those beatings. Weatherwise, it was a beautiful Caribbean day. The sun was shining through the bedroom window where I was, and Mom and our father were arguing about some nonsense in the living room. Truthfully, it was always nonsense. As the argument continued, Mom walked away and came into the bedroom. I guess this upset him greatly and he came charging after her. He picked her up by the scruff of her neck and threw her against the wall. She crashed into the wall and fell to the ground. He simply walked out of the room, walked out the front door, got into the car, and drove off, leaving her there. His mother was always around; she came into the room a few minutes later and said, "I am sure you provoked him and he did what he had to do." Can you imagine that? Instead of comforting her, she told my mother it was her fault!

When our father's older brother came to visit, that was another big deal. He did not like Mom. My grandmother would lock Mom up in the bedroom with instructions not to open the door. If he stayed all day, Mom had to stay put in the room the entire time. When meals were served, my grandmother would take food to Mom in the room. She would open the bedroom door slightly and slide the plate in.

As a child, I dreaded the weekends. The house was always full of people and the liquor would be flowing liberally. Before you knew it, something would be said, someone would get offended, and the fistfights would begin. The house was so violent that I could not bear to watch anything violent on television. Any violence and I would begin to shake uncontrollably.

Our father would beat Mom up so badly she would go home to her parents, only to return in a week or two. My maternal grandfather loved our father with all his heart; when he spoke about him it was always in such glowing terms. I could never understand how he could love someone who used his daughter as a punching bag. I am sure he believed Mom about the beatings, but he would always talk her into returning, and return she did. Back then, spousal abuse was not frowned upon as it is today. Many husbands regularly beat their wives and nothing was ever done about it.

Her beatings continued for years. Finally, when she could not take it any longer, she left for the last time. Instead of going home to her parents, she went to a relative, never to return to her husband's home. Lacking formal education, she did whatever she could to earn a living. She worked hard cooking, cleaning, ironing, taking care of older people, or babysitting—whatever job she found, she did. Our dad refused to support us. When we would tell him we needed food, his response was, "I always have food at my house. If you are hungry, you can come there to eat, but I will not support your mother and her brothers." Whenever he said that to me, I wanted to scream at him, "You horrible bastard! We are hungry and you don't care!" But as a child I knew my place and that I could not talk back to my elders. I never loved him, and his behavior never endeared me to him. I never developed a relationship with him, and that was okay with me.

Fate smiled on Mom through the kindness of a stranger, and she was given the opportunity to come to the United States, leaving her four babies behind with her parents. If she had not left, I am not sure we all would have lived to become adults. When she left, she promised that as soon as she could afford it, she would send for us. We believed her, and she certainly kept her promise.

Upon her arrival in the United States, she got a job as a maid. It was very difficult for her being away from us, but when you are poor, options are few. She had to support us; in the United States, the promise of a better life existed, while where we lived there was no life to speak of. It would be five years before her two older kids would join her, and another three before the younger two came. It took eight years for all her kids to finally reunite with her.

CAN ALZHEIMER'S BE PREVENTED?

When a family member gets this disease, his or her loved ones try so hard to find answers.

I have read and reread books and articles on this disease. I have even taken classes on preventative steps to avoid it. I would do almost anything to be proactive and avoid this dreaded enemy.

Article after article and book after book state that we must stay active, engaged, and alert. If you keep learning and exercising, you can push the full onset of the disease further and further into the future.

Is that true? Is it really that easy? Who knows? If it is, I am already signed up, but on the other hand, this information suggests that perhaps the victims were lax in these areas and thus, in a way, it's their fault they are ill. My God, I hope this is not true!

I often look at Mom and wonder what she, and we, could have done differently that would have prevented this from happening. That being said, this disease is a lot sadder than I first imagined it to be.

Growing up, Mom did not have many friends. She was simply too busy with her goal of trying to create a better life for her children. She had little time for friends, which were a luxury she could ill afford. It seems many people were somewhat indifferent to a young mother of four. We never went to restaurants or took summer vacations, because we could not afford it. Not that we missed those things, because we didn't know we were supposed to have them.

Attending church was always a constant. Of course, it was affordable—i.e., free. At home we never had parties, but guests were readily welcome. Mom believed in sharing what little we had with others.

As soon as I became a teenager, I joined her on Sundays at work. Work was what we knew and what kept her alive.

If this disease was somehow triggered by a lack of socialization and a failure to keep her brain active, then the only thing I can say is shame on it!

THE ONE WE LOST

How can we measure the loss of one so dear and sweet? This terrible ailment has literally stolen another soul. This time it's my mother, my beautiful, wonderful mom who always saw the good in others and tried so hard to live a decent life.

I've been trying to understand how this disease can take hold of someone, set up shop, and fully take over and destroy everything at the expense of its host. This is not a normal parasite. Usually parasites allow their hosts to live, because if the hosts live, they will live too. However, this parasite is different; it just takes over and completely sweeps the entire head clean.

When Mom first became ill, on the off chance we spoke of our father, she would say he never cared for anyone but himself. She was convinced he never loved her. She referred to him as being intellectually gifted but lazy and careless. His needs always came first; he was handsome and told her she was ugly.

She was a single parent with four biracial children, and no one wanted her, or us, around. I am certain this made her angry, but she did a great job of hiding her anger until the disease settled in. When the filter in her brain was removed, all that pent-up anger simply gushed out like a river, flowing out and infecting those closest to her. She lashed out at the people she had worked so hard to protect, and we got the full force of her fury.

No one is safe now from her anger. At times, even strangers get an earful if they come too close. Most of her words now are full of hate and anger; rarely will she say something nice. She was a friendless young lady, and now she has become a friendless old woman.

She lived for her children and, later in life, for her grandchildren. She was fiercely protective of all of us, but, alas, this too was taken away from her way too early in her life.

DAD

I don't have any happy memories of my parents together. To put it mildly, our biological dad was a beast. As a child, I wished he would die, and when he did not die, I wished he would just disappear from our lives forever. I was never fortunate enough to get my first wish. I remembered quite clearly when he left for Germany to work for a rich family. I was the happiest little girl for a few days. Three days later someone saw him and mentioned to us he was back. I did not want to believe it, but sadly for me it was true. He made up a story about why he had to return, but I am sure once those people saw him, they quickly figured out what sort of individual he was and shipped him back home. Thankfully, our parents separated when we were quite young, and although he did not totally disappear, I no longer had to see him on a daily basis.

Even in her illness, Mom can still recall some of the bad things about him. I guess he made such an impression on her that, even if she does not remember clearly, she certainly has some memories of him tucked away in that dying brain of hers.

She told me she saw him just the other day. She has no clue he died a few years ago. He woke up one morning not feeling well, went to the doctor, was admitted to the hospital, had surgery a day later, and never regained consciousness. He died four days later. Now, how is that fair? He never suffered! One would think that someone like him would have to suffer before leaving this world. Of course, he had to die on February 29, 2012, so I am forced to remember the date. Who can forget a leap year day, which comes only once every four years? No one!

I remember saying on the day he died that the world was a much better place without that monster. The day he was buried, I wore a red dress to celebrate his departure to his forever

15

home, wherever that may be. If there is a heaven, and I hope there is one, I pray he does not end up there. If he does, then I don't want to go there at all. I would rather be in hell than be in heaven with him.

WISHING AND HOPING

We have a friend who has multiple sclerosis. We have watched her decline for the past twenty years. When I first met her, she was walking with a cane. A few years later she began to walk with two canes, then a walker. Several years later she was in a wheelchair. Then she slowly lost the use of her hands. Currently, she is unable to move one muscle in her body. She is bedridden, propped up and only able to move her head. She is such a wonderful and pleasant person; in all the years I've known her, I've never once heard her complain.

Each time we have meals with her family, which is a few times each year, she prays and asks God to heal her. She truly believes that one of these days God will listen and heal her. What faith!

When Mom initially got sick, I used to ask God to heal her, but the more I read about this disease, the more I knew there was nothing we, or God, could do for her. In the past few years, I wish I could say I've prayed to God to heal Mom. I have not. I stopped doing that a long time ago. I have no confidence that there is any chance of healing for her. I expect things will continue the way they have been and she will slip further and further away. I also have no faith that science will unlock the mystery of this disease in time to help her. So when I pray, perhaps from a selfish perspective, I ask the Lord in His mercy not to prolong her suffering. I keep reminding Him of the life she had and of how unfair all of this is to her. Is He listening? Does He answer? No, because she is still here and her suffering is being prolonged.

I go through all the what-ifs with Him. I do not believe in promising God anything, because who am I to promise anything? I am just a little speck traveling in this great cosmos, so what

17

can I do for an all-knowing and powerful God? Nothing! Even if I were presumptuous and promised something, I know in my heart I would be incapable of holding up my end of the bargain. However, I keep reminding Him there should be a better way. I tell Him she deserves better, and I keep hoping that one of these days He will have mercy on her. Until then, we impatiently await an answer that never comes.

WHAT IS LIFE?

Growing up, I could never remember a time when Mom did not work. She was the only member of her family who seemed to always have steady employment. If she did not work, we did not eat.

She must have felt enormous pressure to always have employment. It struck me the other day how funny life is. I was going through some paperwork for her and realized the value of her life, at least from a monetary perspective.

Mom has a little black-and-white box where she stores all her important papers. Its measurement is approximately twenty inches in length and twelve inches high. The documents it stores include her passport, birth certificate, social security card, insurance card, and a few other important papers she collected along the way.

She has no stocks, bonds, home, land, or savings. The only things of material value in her life are the contents of this little box. She worked so hard for so many years and has nothing of value to show for it. When she was well, this must have been very upsetting to her. If it were me, I would be upset myself.

In the end, it really does not matter, because when we leave this world, we take nothing with us.

In the game of life, some of us are dealt cruel hands, and having Alzheimer's disease is the cruelest hand of all.

AS TIME GOES BY

I was never a person who counted the years, but that changed once Mom got sick. I count not only the years but the days. I have no choice, because once she became ill, my life as I knew it changed. I believe Mom is in her ninth or tenth year of this disease now.

In the first years, when we did not realize she was ill, the issues were minor. When she first began doing strange things, we attributed it to her getting older. Now, in retrospect, we can see it was the beginning of the end for her. Mind you, I know we all have to die sometime, but there is dying and then there is this disease. To date, it's in a category all its own that is still being defined, at least in my mind.

For me, the years have gone at a snail's pace. Why? It is because every single thing about her illness has changed our lives. I am no longer my own person—her life is now my life. I sort of ceased to exist once she got sick. I am her caretaker; that is my primary role. Everything I do is with her in mind. I seldom do anything for myself. The person I used to be faded into the background. I have not gone on a vacation in years. How can I? I need to be around for her just in case, or we cannot afford it, or we are not comfortable spending the money in case we need to buy her something unexpectedly. I don't think it is selfish of me to want to live my life the way I see fit. It is not fair to me, but I do not figure into this equation; it is all about her and her needs. If I try to do something for myself, I feel guilty. If I don't visit her, I feel guilty. No matter what I do, I feel guilty. I am just a bundle of guilt. Is it so wrong to want my life back? I don't think so, but for now and for all the years that seem to have gone into eternity, I've put my life on hold, not because I wanted to, but because I had no choice!

While one wishes for the best each day, we are not always surprised when the worst rears its ugly head. This illness simply takes and takes, and when you think you have no more to give, it borrows. I used to believe that God is always on time and He shows up. I believe that Mom was a good Christian. In my opinion, somehow God has forgotten about her and, just perhaps, He has missed His mode of transportation—because as far as I am concerned, His timing is off and He has yet to show up. This disease strips one of everything and leaves its victims with nothing. Hope, faith, and whatever else you have are taken and you are left, standing as it were, truly broken.

I have a friend whose father recently died from this disease. He decided to donate his dad's brain to science. I plan on doing the same with Mom. I hope her brain can serve to ease the pain of a child whose parent is being snuffed out by this repugnant parasite.

I was cautioned by one of my friends recently that I must be careful not to die before Mom does. Now that would be an ironic twist of fate! You know the old adage about the green fruit falling off the branch, leaving the ripe one behind and intact (meaning the young dying and leaving the old ones behind). I can actually see this happening, because Mom does not have a care in this world. She has no clue about anything. Therefore, I am assuming she has no stress at all in her life. She is waited on hand and foot and is pampered as much as anyone in her state can be. Without a memory, what is there to worry about?

Sometimes she is happy. We take walks, talk, and do other normal everyday things that people do, although normal is something we will never truly be again.

I never had children, but now I have a child in Mom. I would like to stop time, rewind the clock, and go back to the good old days when she was the only parent I knew and I was her child. She was the one who cared for us and ensured we were safe. How I long for those bygone days, which were not so long ago! I remember those seemingly carefree times so clearly. All of my dreams have slowly slipped into a nightmare, and I know there is no waking up from this one.

Someone asked me, "If you had one wish in life, what would it be?" That is an easy one. With no hesitation, no hemming or hawing, no problem with the sentence structure, I answered, "Give me back my mother minus the disease."

What is life if it lacks the potential to be lived to the fullest? This disease takes that potential away and leaves only an outer shell that resembles the person, but when you look closer, there is absolutely nothing inside that shell. Not only does Alzheimer's take away the essence of who you are, but it leaves behind a placeholder to remind the family that something precious is now lost and will never be replaced.

When Mom says something funny, we laugh. We do so because there is nothing else to do. Tears flow now like water, because that is just the way it is. Living a life with her makes our hearts break constantly. I want my mother back!

SUMMER 2005

In the summer of 2005, I relocated Mom from the Brooklyn apartment where she had lived for many years. The apartment was a Section 8 housing project (government-subsidized, low-income) that was not as bad as some other Section 8 housing. There was a doorman 24/7, which was something unheard of in this type of building. The neighborhood was not the best, but it was not the worst either. Mom knew a few people in the building and made friends with all the guards. Each day she would stop by and speak to the guards and anyone else who was sitting in the lobby.

Between stints of assisting my siblings with childcare, she had lived in the apartment building for more than twenty years. My main reason for moving her was she kept complaining that the people who lived on her floor were not very friendly. She talked about a mean dog that was allowed to roam the floor, and no one could take the elevator if he was in the hallway. She told me about several instances when people would knock on her door in the middle of the night. By far the most annoying thing to her was that someone kept urinating on the door. I never understood why someone would urinate on her door, but several years later it would become abundantly clear to me that these were the beginning signs of Mom's illness. She kept complaining until finally I spoke to my husband, and we made the decision to get her out of Brooklyn and find somewhere closer to us, in New Jersey.

My husband and I had a long discussion about whether to rent or buy a house for her. In 2005, the real estate market in New Jersey was soaring. We wanted to find a nice place for her to live. More importantly, I wanted Mom to have something she had never had before: her own house. Moving her meant moving my sister Sally, and her children also. We could not afford another home in the town we live in because the prices were too high.

We were looking for a quaint town that was safe and had an easy commute to New York City for Sally because of her job. We wanted a house with at least three bedrooms, with a lawn and garden for Mom to work in, that was within walking distance to shopping and kindergarten for my niece Tara, since Mom never learned to drive. My husband and I explored several communities and houses on our own, but we realized it was not going to work unless Mom and Sally liked the house we chose. This made the process much longer than we had planned.

For several months, our routine on Sunday morning was the same: My husband and I drove to Brooklyn to pick up Mom, Sally, and the kids. We then drove back to New Jersey to look at houses. It was tiring, and one Sunday my husband announced it was the last Sunday he would go out and that we had to decide that day which house we would purchase for Mom. Prior to that Sunday, we had put offers on two separate residences, but neither offer was accepted.

We saw a couple of houses that Sunday, and on the following Tuesday we put an offer on a three-bedroom, one-bath house in Middlesex County. My husband and I had made a couple of trips at night to the town to make sure it was safe.

The offer was accepted, and several months later they moved. I was so happy for Mom! I thought to myself, *Finally she has a home where she can relax and enjoy life.*

The house was built on a corner lot with a tiny sliver for a backyard, but there were two large side yards and a lovely front yard. Mom went about transforming the yard into beautiful gardens. There were a couple of bushes she did not like in the front yard; one had huge thorns on it, and she was extremely concerned that my niece Tara could hurt herself if she touched it, so in nothing flat those bushes were out of there!

The side yard to the left of the house became an array of gorgeous colors with many beautiful flowering plants. In front of the house, to one side of the staircase, a rose garden soon blossomed with a cluster of yellow, white, pink, and red roses. On the other side of the stairs, irises and other greener, smaller flowering bushes began to appear. Closer to the street, there was a small garden encircled with rocks where she planted different kinds of lilies. She spent the vast majority of her time outside tending her gardens. She was always cutting, pruning, digging, and enhancing the soil. There was a small brick patio on the side of the house where she had potted plants of all kinds. There was a storage shed on the far side of the property where she built up the soil next to the shed and planted an array of exotic flowers and bushes. She told me some time later that many people would stop in their cars and compliment her on her beautiful gardens.

DAY CARE 2006

Tara was three and a half when Mom moved into her new home. At that time, Mom was her full-time caregiver. To this day, it is my belief that Mom loved her grandchild even more than her own children. Tara was her entire life. She referred to her as her daughter and spoiled her rotten. Mom and Sally used to have disagreements about how to raise Tara. If Sally said "A" was correct, Mom disagreed and said "B," and then "B" it was. She always had the last word when it came to Tara.

When Tara turned four, it was decided she should go to an outside day care for a few hours each day. Mom found a day care that was run out of a local church three blocks from the house and registered Tara. The day care owner was also looking for a caregiver for the babies, and Mom took the job. We all believed she took the job to be with Tara. Things went great for a few weeks, but then Mom began complaining about the owner of the day care center.

The owner's daughter, who was a year older than Tara, was a full-time student at the day care. According to Mom, the child was allowed to have the run of the place and would take no direction from those in charge. She began to have fights with the owner regarding her daughter. One day, Tara had a toy and the owner's daughter forcefully took it away. Mom took it back and returned it to Tara. There was a disagreement between Mom and the owner and, according to Mom, the owner made Tara give the toy back to her daughter. Mom came home and said she would not return to the day care center; for the rest of the week, neither she nor Tara went to day care. The following week, Mom returned to work as if nothing had happened.

A few weeks later, the complaints resumed. I kept reminding Mom she did not have to work there if she did not wish to do so. She kept saying she needed the money. "What money?" I inquired. She was paid minimum wage. She later confessed she really loved the babies and wanted to take care of them. I told her if she wanted to take care of the babies, then she would have to learn to let certain things go and try not to complain about everything.

A month later, she had a significant disagreement with one of the workers over a very trivial matter. She began criticizing the young lady harshly, to the point of calling her terrible names. I could not understand why Mom was being so critical. It did not matter if it was significant or insignificant; everything seemed to get to her and bother her. She would talk about the smallest thing for days.

Mom was the sweetest person you could ever hope to meet. One of my brother's friends, Jim, told him he envied him because of our mother. He wished his mom was like ours.

One night when we were still living in Brooklyn, Mom saw a homeless person going through the garbage cans in front of the building. She ran to the kitchen and made a sandwich, but by the time she was finished with the sandwich, the gentleman was a couple of blocks away from the apartment building. I watched from the window as she ran down the street to catch up with the man, only to return to the apartment several minutes later, sandwich in hand; he had refused to take it. I asked what had happened and her response was, "Oh well, he must have had a bad experience with someone else and refused to take the meal."

Mom's generosity would sometimes border on the dangerous. She would invite total strangers to the apartment for meals. Once, a gentleman showed up at the church we were attending and she invited him home to lunch. When he left, she told him if he ever needed a meal, he could just drop by. He must have had problems with metaphoric language, because for the next year or so, he would routinely drop by a couple of times per week. Mom had two jobs, so she left home early in the morning and returned at night. At times, this man would appear when she was at work. Because we always lived in bad neighborhoods, the front door to the building was always unlocked and he would just walk in, walk up the stairs, and ring the bell. Of course, we would answer the door because we knew him and did not want to be rude.

After a while, he began to make me feel extremely uncomfortable. I recall several times he came at 10:30 at night and would just sit down. Part of the living room doubled as a bedroom, and at that hour of the night it became problematic. It did not matter how many times we said we had school the next day; he would continue to sit. There was always a strong smell of liquor on him. Subsequently, I made Mom speak to one of the church elders and ask them to tell him not to come around that late at night. Thereafter, he stopped the routine. To say the least, I was relieved. Sometime later we learned he was homeless.

Working two jobs meant Mom was always on the subway. One night when she got home, she told me she had given away her last five dollars on the train ride home. When I inquired further, she said someone on the train was asking for money to buy dinner. She gave the person one dollar, but he told her he wanted Chinese food and that one dollar was not enough. Most of us would then ask him to return the dollar, deflating an expectation of more, and then advise him to get off the train while the train was still in motion. Mom said she felt bad and gave him five dollars. It was all the money she had left for the week.

Mom was kind all her life. In contrast, here she was in 2006 having long, drawn-out fights with her employer and other staff members over insignificant issues. When I suggested that she leave instead of getting all worked up over little things, she reacted angrily and accused me of taking sides against her. I tried to explain that I did not know anyone at the day care center and there were no sides to take. She promptly refused to discuss the issue and walked away in a huff, not speaking to me for about two hours thereafter.

She continued to go to the day care center, and as the weeks passed the complaints increased even more. I attempted to listen and not respond, because it wasn't my wish to upset her. Finally, after another few months, she came home and announced she was never going back to the day care center, and that is exactly what she did! We never found out what happened.

Because the day care center was close by, some of the workers walked past the house each day. Mom would complain about them even then. She said if she was in the garden, they would look away to avoid eye contact and not say hello to her. She believed this was done to spite and upset her. I told her she should ignore them, but she did not take my advice. I secretly suspected she went outside at certain times of the day when the workers were passing by to see if they would say hello, and when they did not, she found it necessary to complain.

Mom was so angry with the day care center owner and the workers that she never bothered to collect her final paycheck.

MY NIECE TARA

From birth, Tara became Mom's world. As Mom sank into whatever was going on in her head, we noticed her behavior toward Tara began to change. She became very impatient with her and frequently became quite angry for no reason. If Mom called Tara and she did not respond immediately, Mom would scream at her and call her names. In her anger, she began telling Tara she was a little rat. When Tara tried to respond, Mom would scream at the top of her lungs, "Shut up! If you don't shut up, I will rip your face off!" Her behavior became very disturbing.

On several occasions when I witnessed this behavior, I told Mom this was not acceptable behavior toward a child; she told me to mind my own business. Tara became very confused because her relationship with Mom had always been loving.

Mom's new personality became rather unnerving, for both Sally and Tara, neither of them knowing what to do to keep the angry Mom away.

We took Mom to the doctor and explained what was going on. He recommended a brain scan. When the results were read, he told us he saw "minor" changes in her brain but nothing of significance. He said there was nothing much to worry about. However, from one day to the next, we were unsure which of her personalities would show up. It was really difficult to deal with her. We thought that maybe she had become bipolar, but this was an assumption on our part, since the doctor had said there was nothing to worry about. Her personality had changed and we had no logical explanation for it.

The word "hate" came more frequently as the word "like" all but disappeared from her vocabulary. It didn't matter who you were; if you did something that bothered her, she would express her hatred in no uncertain terms. I remembered talking to her one day about someone from my childhood and she suddenly interjected, "I hate him so much that, if given the opportunity, I would kill him. He is a horrible man." "Kill"—now that was a new word to add to "hate" in her vocabulary. When I told her not to talk like that, she just screamed at me and told me that I liked to meddle in people's business and I should learn not to poke my nose where it did not belong.

She also began saying no one cared about her and she was living like "a dog" in her home. According to her, she was not included in anything and was a stranger to everyone. She would cry and cry, and no matter what was said no one could console her. Every day she would find something to cry about. We all were trying to please her, but no matter what we did, she took it the wrong way and it became a problem.

The week after Mom told me not to poke my nose into people's business, I picked her up to take her to church. I am not sure what happened in the house that morning, but once she got into the car she refused to speak to me. No matter what I said, she did not respond; she just looked out the car window like I was not there. The drive to church was over thirty minutes. When we arrived, she spoke to members of the church like absolutely nothing had occurred on the drive there. Her mood was jovial. We had lunch, and there too everything seemed fine. After lunch, we got back in the car for the ride home, and I assumed she would be in a much better mood, seeing as she had been so happy and talkative while we were at church. I soon learned I had made the wrong assumption.

I began speaking to her once we got back in the car, but the person who got into the car was not the person I had seen in church. That shadowy mood returned, and when we got back to her house, she promptly went to her room and never emerged. To this day, I have no clue what made her so upset.

KINDERGARTEN

In 2007, Tara began school. By this time, Mom had made a couple of friends in the neighborhood. Growing up, Mom had always been working and had no time to make friends, so I was overjoyed that she now had friends. It was nice that she knew a few people now and could discuss the events of the day with them.

Mom would walk Tara the five blocks to school each day. She always held on to her hand on the way to school. Once they arrived at the school, the children had to stand in line by grades. Mom would not let her get in line until the bullhorn announced the kids had to begin the march to enter the building.

One of the friends she made was another grandmother who had to drop off her grandchild at school each day. Mom and this lady would talk for hours after the kids went into the building. Her new friend kept inviting her out to lunch and other places, but for some strange reason Mom always found an excuse not to go. I assume that because she did not have friends outside of church, she did not feel comfortable going.

Shortly after Tara began school, Mom developed another habit: standing at the window with the shades open. She looked out through the open shades for hours. She also developed a habit of calling the local police department. She had all kinds of complaints and things for the police to investigate. I kept telling her she had to stop calling them. Her response was, "I've never made a false report to the police." Then she relayed that on this particular morning, she had been looking out the window when she saw two kids walking along; she assumed they were going to school and that perhaps they were brother and sister. According to her, she saw a van drive up and the person in the van began speaking to the little girl. At this point, the little boy began walking a little faster and was now ahead of the girl. Mom had no idea what the conversation was about, but she decided the person in the van was trying to kidnap the little girl. She called 911 to report what she was seeing. After the phone call, the police arrived within minutes. She was very pleased with herself, because she now knew the kids were safe. The unknown driver went on his way and she had saved the day.

She called the police often. It got so bad that I told her if she did not stop calling 911, the police department would start charging her money for calling. That did nothing to stop her calls; she told me I had money and would be able to pay the fine.

THE POLICE AGAIN

In the spring of 2008, Mom was still taking care of Tara and walking her to school on a daily basis. Sally had gotten Mom an easy-to-use cell phone, just in case there was an emergency and she needed to get in touch with us. It was midweek and Mom went to pick Tara up. She always arrived at least fifteen minutes before the door opened to let the kids out. She was overly cautious because she feared Tara might wander off if she arrived late. So it was better in her estimation to be extra early.

On their return journey home, Tara customarily skipped along on the sidewalk. Mom allowed her to skip ahead, but at the end of each block she had to wait for Mom before attempting to cross the street. Upon arriving at the house, Mom checked her purse and discovered she did not have the keys to open the door. She immediately called the police and explained what had happened. When the officers arrived, they walked around the house and found a window in the kitchen that was slightly open. One of them asked if there was a ladder available so he could climb up and open the window to gain access to the house. Mom told him there was a ladder in the storage shed. He retrieved the ladder, climbed up, and opened the window. He used a knife to cut the screen off. It was decided that they would put Tara through the open window because she was tiny; his partner passed Tara up to him, and he in turn put her through the now open screen. She climbed in, stepped into the sink, and maneuvered her way from the countertop to the floor, then to the front door, which she unlocked. Once inside the house, Mom called me to tell me what had happened. She thought the entire thing was so funny.

I told her that, to avoid something like this happening in the future, she should hide an extra door key in Tara's backpack,

34

just in case. She refused. She was wary that someone might take it from the backpack and have access to the house. In her mind, that would be a bigger disaster than calling the police and gaining access through a window. When I asked how the person would know which house the key would fit, she said, "People have ways of finding things out."

THE LAND

Since the late 1980s/early 1990s, I've arranged for Mom to go to her former home in the Caribbean every two years to visit her family. In 2009, she began talking about purchasing a piece of land in her hometown. It was the land where she grew up. Her childhood home belonged to her parents, but the land was owned by someone else. Her parents were supposed to pay rent on the land, but after the landlord passed away, his extended family never bothered to collect the rent. Apparently, the family had a long-running dispute that seemed unresolvable and no one wanted the other to be accused of taking money from the tenants, so it remained in a state of limbo.

On one of Mom's visits, she mentioned to one of the local attorneys that she was interested in purchasing the piece of property that the house stood on, plus two adjacent lots. He agreed to assist—for a fee, of course. Somehow the word got out that she was interested in purchasing the land. The neighbor living across the walkway from her parents' home had moved there some forty-five years earlier. He found out about the pending purchase and decided the land should not be sold and tried to prevent the sale. He was a farmer, and in the past he had planted on nearby lots that he did not own. Once he heard about Mom's interest in the property, he decided he would cultivate the two vacant lots she was interested in acquiring.

My uncle told Mom what the neighbor had done, and she really got angry. She would speak of the land constantly and how the farmer was attempting to forcefully take something to which her parents were entitled. She was now convinced if he continued to cultivate the land, it would become much more difficult to purchase the three lots.

When she spoke to the attorney, she never envisioned that anyone would know about the pending land sale. I had taken no steps to initiate the purchase of the land, as I was convinced the attorney would take payments but not render the expected services.

As Mom's obsession with the land grew, I decided that it might relieve some of her anxiety if my husband and I actually began the purchase process. Mom contacted the attorney, who requested $7,000 US dollars, estimating this should suffice for the research and purchase. Because her family had lived on the land for almost ninety years, he believed back taxes would be the only impediment to acquiring the land.

Once the money was sent, her anxiety grew exponentially. Each day when I called, the topic of the land came up along with the farmer's name. She always mentioned how much she hated him and how if she ever saw him she would kill him. Something in me felt this was no idle threat and that she meant every word.

A much darker side to Mom's personality now emerged. From time to time it truly scared me and left me wondering, *What is happening to her? Where is this anger coming from? What can we do to make it go away?*

As the sale of the land dragged on, her anger grew stronger. We tried to contact the attorney several times to no avail. Finally, she asked one of her brothers to visit the attorney's office. My uncle was told another $7,500 was needed to continue the research. He was given a copy of a paper that showed the sale of the land in the 1800s. The piece of paper had a crown stamp on it to prove it was a legal document. However, years later we found out the piece of paper was worthless. I told Mom we did not have the additional money, and so the purchase of the land, like many of her dreams, died. After this she added the attorney to her "hate" list.

BIRTHDAY

In February 2009, I decided to throw Mom a birthday party. I invited approximately forty people for a private party at a local restaurant. I thought it would be a good idea to give her something she'd never had. Our excitement, however, was tempered because of her growing mental issues. I decided I would give her a little happiness while her mind was still somewhat intact. At the time, I was hoping she would remember her birthday a year later. I requested no gifts because I wanted it to be a celebration for her, not about the gifts she could get from the guests.

On the day of the party, she was in a very good mood. I was so grateful for this. Some of the guests brought gifts anyway. As she walked around the semiprivate area at the restaurant trying to have conversations with people, I noticed she was having trouble expressing what she wanted to say. I chalked it up to her excitement about the party.

The party was an overwhelming success. For a few hours, Mom seemed happy. I sat and watched her go from table to table thanking everyone for coming and trying to keep up with the conversations. All the while I kept thinking that Mom was becoming a stranger to us and wondering how much longer I would be able to go on this emotional ride with her.

CANCER

A few months after the birthday party in 2009, I received a disturbing phone call from Sally. I was at work, and as soon as I picked up the phone I could hear an anxious tone in her voice.

Mom had woken up that morning, and on her way downstairs Sally noticed a small amount of blood on her nightgown in the breast area. I guess Mom was so shocked that she showed it to Sally. Nothing else needed to be said; I was convinced I knew what it was. A few years earlier, one of my friends had the same thing happen to her. She too called me at work and relayed the story in the same manner as Sally had. Several tests later, my friend was informed she had breast cancer.

I told Sally Mom had breast cancer, and she told me not to say such a thing. I relayed my friend's experience, and I could hear the fear creep into Sally's voice as she asked, "What should I do?" After instructing her not to divulge anything to Mom until there was confirmation, I asked that she set up a doctor's appointment.

The appointment was made and the doctor conducted several tests. Then the waiting game began—it felt like a million years passed as we waited for the results.

A week or so after the tests, Mom called my office crying. I could barely understand what she was saying. It was a midmorning call, and it took me several minutes to calm her down enough to understand her. When she was calm enough to speak, she said she had just received a call from the medical center and the caller told her the tests confirmed she had breast cancer.

I was livid that the doctor's office had allowed such a terrible piece of information to be disseminated via telephone rather than a personal consultation with the doctor. She was given another doctor's contact details to call and get a treatment plan in place. The first doctor's office may have employed great diagnosticians, but they were extremely insensitive. I wanted to give these troglodytes a piece of my mind, but my husband calmed me down by reminding me the damage was already done and we should concentrate on Mom's treatment instead.

On receiving the diagnosis of breast cancer, something terrible seemed to happen to Mom. It was as if a light switch went from on to off in an instant. She was forgetful before, but all of a sudden it seemed she could not remember anything. A couple of weeks later, I accompanied her to the new doctor's office for the follow-up visit. I waited for a very long time in the reception area for her return. Finally, she appeared at the end of a long hallway. She was leaning against the wall, slowly sliding herself along it, seemingly exhausted and lost. I sat there stunned and unable to move for a few seconds. What was the matter with Mom? We had come into the office, the nurse had called her, she had accompanied the nurse, and now, not one hour later, she was unable to find her way back to the reception area.

Upon seeing me, her face lit up with a smile. I got up from the chair and walked swiftly toward her. When I finally reached her, she told me she had forgotten how to get back to the reception area and was afraid I would leave her at the center. Then she began to cry. I reassured her I would never leave her, but that did not seem to help; she just continued to cry.

Less than one month later, she had surgery to remove the lump in her breast. Afterward, we were assured by the physicians the cancer was in the early stages.

Mom summarily rejected post-surgery radiation therapy. The doctor suggested an alternative treatment involving taking pills daily for five years, but this was met with the same resistance as the radiation therapy. It was Mom's unassailable conviction that if she was cancer-free, then she needed no further treatment. I did not attempt to force her to do otherwise.

Her belief seems to have borne out. As of this writing, the cancer has not recurred.

THE DOOR

One night in the beginning of spring 2009, I got a frantic phone call from Sally. "Mother broke the back door!" she exclaimed.

All at once she had my full attention. "What do you mean she broke the back door?"

Sally said that when she came home from work that evening, the entire glass panel on the back door was broken. Mom had locked herself out of the house earlier in the day, and instead of calling one of us, she broke the glass panel and unlocked the door by putting her hand through the opening.

When I had spoken to Mom earlier that day, she never mentioned the incident. According to Sally, Mom took Tara to school and, upon her return home, discovered she had forgotten her keys and cell phone in the house. With no way to enter the house, she went to the garden, got a medium-size rock, and broke the glass pane on the door to gain entrance.

I asked Sally to put Mom on the phone. Once she got on, I asked her if it was true about the door. She replied, "Yes, it is, but not to worry. The door was not real glass, so it's fine."

I asked her why she hadn't gone next door to the neighbor and asked to use his phone to call me at work, as I had an extra set of keys and would have come over to let her in. The next-door neighbor and his wife were both retired and were usually at home most of the day. Mom used to have conversations with them all the time while working in the garden, so it would not have been far-fetched for her to ask them to use their phone in an emergency.

"I don't want them to think I am stupid," she said.

"Who cares what they think?" I asked.

"I do," she responded.

At this point I asked her if she knew how much it would cost to replace the door. "Don't bother me with that," she said, and went on to say that I had the money and could easily replace the door. Frustrated, she insisted she didn't want to talk about the door anymore and handed the phone back to Sally.

We were upset, but the damage was done. I told Sally to keep the kitchen door locked going forward, just in case someone tried to enter the house through the broken door. Several weeks later I replaced the door; the new door cost $850. I tried in vain to discuss this incident with Mom, but as far as she was concerned, it was a closed subject.

THE SQUIRREL

Shortly after the door incident, Mom kept telling me that something was moving in the walls of the house. She kept saying that, during the day, whatever it was would run around in the walls of the house, starting from the dining room wall and circling the entire house.

When I went to the house, I asked her to explain exactly what she was hearing. To illustrate, she pointed to the middle of the wall and said, "It starts around here and runs the entire length of the house in circles, and it's driving me crazy."

I tried to explain that I could understand something going into the attic or moving into the basement, but I could not see how something could move into the wall and run around in circles. I even told her if something had indeed moved into the wall, it would run up and down rather than in a circle. I said perhaps she was hearing whatever it was going up and down, not in circles. She replied, "I know what I am hearing and I know it is in circles. You can think what you want, but I know the truth." A few days later, she told me the creature was now waking her up at night because it was making so much noise.

I could not get her to understand that perhaps she was mistaken. No matter how I tried to explain that creatures, like humans, need to sleep and that whatever she was hearing could not be up twenty-four hours a day, seven days a week. She insisted she was right and I was wrong. When I went to visit her a week later, she took me outside the house and pointed out a small opening next to the gutter where she believed the creature had gained access to the walls. Just to calm her down, I called an exterminator and asked him to set up a trap next to the small opening.

The exterminator visited several times to check the trap with the same disappointing results: nothing in it. After four months with no creature in sight, I asked the exterminator to remove the trap.

To his credit, when I inquired about payment for his services, he said there was no charge, as his policy was "no creature, no payment."

A few weeks after the trap's removal, Mom called me at work very excited. The mystery about the circling creature in the wall was solved. She had been outside—as she was most of the time during the spring, summer, and fall months—and she just happened to look up and saw a squirrel coming out of the tiny space in the gutter. She was positive this was the squirrel that was giving her so many sleepless nights and so much daytime annoyance.

"Did you actually see the squirrel come out of the tiny space?" I asked.

She was sure it had come from the little hole. "Now, how do we get rid of him?" she asked me.

I explained that the trap we had set earlier yielded nothing. She would hear none of it and was determined to arrange a rendezvous between the squirrel and its maker. I assume she tried throwing things at the squirrel, because a few weeks later she told me her sneaker was stuck in the gutter.

Now that she knew there was a squirrel taking up residence in the house (at least, that was what she thought), she was no longer afraid of the noise, but continued plotting to evict this unwelcome, nonpaying guest.

Several weeks passed after the first sighting. One Saturday while visiting me at my house, she said she needed to speak to me, but before she did I had to promise not to think she was crazy.

"Remember the squirrel that is living in the wall?" she asked.

Who could forget him? He had been the topic of conversation for months. I politely said I did.

She went on to say, "Well, for the past couple of weeks, I think he has been laughing at me."

I must have had a funny look on my face, because she said, "There you go thinking I am crazy." I reminded her I had said nothing. She answered, "You don't have to, because the look on your face gave your feelings away."

"What do you mean when you say the squirrel is laughing at you?"

She paused for a few seconds, then looked away. "For the past few weeks, when I take Tara to school, the squirrel sits on the electrical wire running in front of the house, and as soon as I exit the door, he begins making funny noises that sound like laughter." She said he would also wait until she returned from dropping Tara off and start the laughter anew.

I tried to explain that when squirrels feel threatened, they make sounds to drive away what they believe to be a threat. This did absolutely nothing to dissuade her from her belief that this belligerent rodent was laughing at her. I was at a loss to figure out why she was thinking the way she was, and no matter what I told her, she truly believed the rodent was teasing her. What would make her believe that a tiny squirrel had the sense to laugh at her?

About a month later she called me at work laughing hysterically. When I picked up the phone I thought she was crying, until she finally calmed down enough to relate to me her funny story.

The previous night there had been a power outage in the neighborhood. She had been watching television when suddenly there was a big boom. She ran to the window and saw the overhead transformer on the power line smoking. The power was gone.

A few hours later, the maintenance crew had everything up and running again. The following morning when taking Tara to school, she saw fur, then the tail portion of a squirrel. Apparently, a squirrel had somehow gotten into the transformer and . . . well, you get the picture. She could barely contain her joy because she was convinced the deceased beast was her previous tormentor. "He is gone, and good riddance," she said as she continued to laugh. How could she think that this was the squirrel that had supposedly bothered her for months?

Her joy was short-lived, because a couple of days later she called and said there was another squirrel in the wall. Mom thought it was the baby of the one who was now dead. No matter how much I told her what she was saying did not make sense, I could not change her mind. Her mind was made up and there was nothing I could say or do to change it. She knew the truth despite what I said. I now truly believed she was losing her mind.

THE BIG TREE NEXT DOOR

There is a huge tree located on the right side of the house on our neighbor's property. A couple of the branches overhang our property. These branches hang close to Tara's bedroom. For over a year, Mom was obsessed with the branches. Each time I visited I got a new perspective on this persistent subject.

She insisted the tree was a danger and that in a storm it could trap—or worse, kill—Tara in her room. I kept reminding her that the tree did not belong to us; she insisted I cut it down. I tried reasoning with her, explaining that because it was not ours, I would get in trouble if I tried to cut it down.

I tried to console her by telling her the tree seemed quite healthy, so there was nothing to worry about. Each time the subject came up, though, Mom had something new to report. She said that during minor rain and wind, the branches could be heard scraping along the rooftop. I insisted that even if the branches hit the roof, it was nothing to worry about.

Her concern and obsession grew even worse as the weeks passed. I had to go to the house on a few occasions just to relieve her concern and look at the tree myself. The issue simply grew larger. Adding insult to injury, she now insisted the squirrel was still running around in the wall and would now go on the tree when he saw her and make that funny laughter-like noise.

Just to keep her calm, I began calling her several times a day just to reassure her that all was fine. Finally, she told me if I didn't cut the tree down, both the tree and squirrel would drive her insane.

A week later, she was happy to report she had spoken to the owner of the house and he had given her permission to trim the two offending branches that were hanging over the bedroom. I was told to call someone and make the necessary arrangements.

I complied and contacted a tree-trimmer, who quoted a price of $750 for the work. I told Mom I could not afford to have the branches removed and this made her very upset. She raised her voice and insisted the amount was small and she knew I could afford it. The tree branches and the squirrel remained the bane of her existence.

THE NEW FRIEND

In the summer of 2010, as Mom's behavior kept morphing into uncharted territory and her memory grew more fragile than ever, we decided it would be a very good idea for someone to be with her at all times. Mom always had trust issues, and she was reluctant to have a stranger in the house while Sally was at work.

So distrustful was Mom of strangers that she never allowed my niece to go on playdates at anyone's house. To be fair, she didn't play favorites, as she never allowed anyone to come to our house for playdates either. One of her favorite mantras was: "I don't trust people as far as I can throw them."

We contacted our cousin Cindy and asked if she would be interested in relocating to the United States for an extended stay. She agreed. Cindy had previously visited and Mom was quite fond of her. My cousin received a six-month visa and came to stay with Mom.

Cindy, who is shy, had known Mom when she was well. However, in her current state, that nice person had long moved on and the "new" her was here to stay. We told Cindy that Mom had changed a lot, but she still agreed to come and assist us. Cindy moved into a home that was practically a war zone. Every day Mom would routinely complain about Sally, probably just after having her morning coffee or tea. At least three times per week there was a shouting match, with Mom being the primary culprit. If I didn't know better, I would say the movie *Monsters, Inc.* was inspired by this situation.

At the house, no one could have a phone conversation in private. If the phone rang and the person took the phone into another room, Mom became convinced the conversation was about her and nothing good was being said. She began locking herself in her room when Sally came home from work and would not come out until Sally went to bed or left the house.

Sally could not speak to Mom at all. If she tried, Mom would just scream at her and tell her what a horrible bitch she was. At every opportunity, Mom let Sally know that she hated her.

Mom began telling Cindy that no one loved her and we were trying to get rid of her. She truly believed that somehow we were planning to harm her in some way. Adding fuel to the raging fire, Mom now developed a brand-new habit to add to her growing repertoire: She began to tear and rip apart her clothing. This began occurring more frequently.

There were two dehumidifiers in the basement that we kept running to keep the moisture out. When they filled up with water, instead of emptying them out as she used to, she began storing the water in the washing machine. When this was brought to my attention, I advised her not to put the water in the washing machine, but she insisted she was just trying to save on the water bill and refused to listen. She also started washing clothes on a daily basis, rather than washing based on how much dirty laundry there was, even if there were only two pieces of clothing. Even though she was now washing on a daily basis, she refused to touch anything that belonged to Sally. Sally began fussing about the rising costs of running the house, and Mom complained about everything else.

Mom now talked about going back to her childhood home and told me she would be better off dead than living the way she thought she was living. Nothing I told her sank into her head. Her reality was certainly different from mine, and I could see she was now truly sick. Her statement about being dead made me very sad. She continued to say she had a dog's life and lived like an unwanted dog in the house. She could never have a conversation without crying hysterically. The more reassurance I gave her, the more she cried.

There was, however, another side to Mom. While in public, she retained that sweet, wonderful persona she'd had previously, which she closeted with surgical precision once she returned to the house. She now began telling anyone who would listen how horrible Sally was. There was no logical explanation for her attitude toward Sally.

I took her back to the doctor, a number of tests were done, and we got the same response from the doctor as we had the last time: "We see some changes in her brain, but we believe this is part of the aging process." Mom was never officially diagnosed with Alzheimer's disease, as this diagnosis is only rendered at death when doctors can look at the brain and see the damage the disease has inflicted.

THE STORY

For most of her life, Mom was very religious. She partici-
pated in several activities at church. She sang solos and was
a member of the choir for many years. When she moved to New
Jersey, I was attending a small church and she accompanied me
each Saturday. The church did not have a choir, but Mom volunteered to do whatever she could to help out. Part of the church
service included telling the children Bible stories. Mom told a
story at least once per month.

As her behavior changed and she became more unpredictable,
I persistently attempted to stop her from doing activities at
church. However, she signed up for the storytelling without
my knowledge. I found out a couple of days before she
was scheduled to tell the story that coming Saturday. I was
concerned that things would get out of hand and wanted to know
in advance what story she was going to tell. I called her the day
before church and asked about the story. She told me what she
was going to do and I asked if she had practiced the story. She
responded, "Yes, I did." I reminded her there was a time limit
for telling the story and she said, "I know the limit."

On Saturday when we were driving to church, I again
reminded her several times about the time limit for the story,
which was five minutes. "It is all under control," she assured
me. When it was almost time for the story, just before she got
up to take her position at the front of the congregation, I raised
five fingers and whispered it to her as she passed my pew: "Five
minutes." She smiled and winked at me as she made her way to
a waiting chair.

Initially she was fine and told the story with only a few little
mistakes. But then she droned on and on, repeating what she had
already said. Five minutes quickly turned into six, then nine,

minutes. Sally and I were sitting in the same pew, and after ten minutes she whispered in my ear, "You have to go up there and end the story yourself."

I could not embarrass Mom like that in front of everyone. By this time, Sally was turning a deep shade of red because she was embarrassed. I raised my hand just a little and waved to see if Mom would look at me, but she did not. I lowered my head and prayed she would stop. Finally, after fifteen minutes her story mercifully ended. I felt so bad for her because she had no idea she had taken that much time. When she passed me to go back to her seat, she once again winked at me, sat down, and just smiled. From her reaction, I could tell she thought she had done a great job.

At the conclusion of the church service, I spoke to the person in charge of the schedule and begged her not to allow Mom to tell a story ever again. I made her promise if Mom signed up for anything, I would be notified and I would fulfill the task, or I would find someone else if I was unavailable. That was the last time Mom did anything in church.

ANOTHER HABIT

In the fall of 2010, Mom acquired another habit. Sally kept telling me Mom was hanging the bedsheets on the windows. This was a new activity, and because her behavior was ever changing, I told Sally, "Just leave her alone and don't say anything to her." I wanted to see what was going on myself.

I visited Mom that weekend. When I went to her room, I found she had hung bedsheets all over the walls and windows. She had run a string along the wall and added some nails to the wall and hung the sheets on them. "Why are the sheets on the wall?" I asked her.

"The room is cold, and this helps keep the room less drafty," she replied.

This behavior was quite odd, and even though she seemed to be acquiring more behavioral issues, I didn't want to think she was losing her mind. I always assumed because she was getting older that perhaps this was part of her aging process. However, we were concerned enough at this point that I took her to the doctor again. When we explained what was going on, the doctor said that maybe she was bored and not to worry about it. After we got the doctor's explanation, I decided he knew best and I should not be overly concerned because I had enough to worry about when it came to Mom. I decided to just let her hang the sheets.

I am not a fan of modern medicine because I believe doctors are too intrusive when it comes to treating people. They perform unnecessary tests and dispense medication like candy; if Mom did not wish to go to the doctor, I did not insist she go. I knew she did not have anything growing in her brain such as a tumor. So I kept telling myself, and the rest of the family, her behavior was just as the doctor stated: part of the aging process.

After a few months, her room looked like a Bedouin tent bazaar. Sally kept telling me to make her take the sheets down, but no matter what we said the sheets stayed put, only to be taken down, washed, and rehung.

I kept telling myself this was just another phase she was going through because she could not work in her beautiful gardens in the winter. I was convinced that once spring arrived the behavior would correct itself.

And so spring came and her flowers bloomed. Mom's garden grew. She was almost her old self. Once again, her garden was one of the most beautiful in the neighborhood. With the warmer weather, I was hoping the bedsheets would come off the walls and windows, but they never did. So, we learned to avoid the subject of the hanging bedsheets. Why talk about something that would only get her upset?

ADDITIONAL HABITS

In the fall of 2010, Mom acquired another habit. She loved to sew and would make several beautiful outfits for herself during the year. She had learned how to sew at a very young age. My grandmother taught her. (I also learned how to sew from my grandmother.) Years ago I bought Mom a sewing machine, and even though she was unwell, I continued to purchase fabric for her to make clothes. Now once she was finished with a piece, she began to rip it apart. Once this was done, she started the process all over again.

When I visited her, she would have pieces of fabric pinned together in an endless stream all over her room. When I asked when she would finish the project, she would reply, "Don't worry about it—I will get to it eventually." The same dress or top would be sewn repeatedly, but once completed, it never seemed to be exactly what she had envisioned and she would do it over again. Sewing was an activity she had enjoyed for decades, and now she could not even manage a few simple stitches.

In addition to the fabric, I also bought her many lovely dresses; she began taking these dresses apart as well. She would cut some fabric off the top portion of the dress, and when she tried to put it back together, it never seemed to be what she wanted so she had to take it apart again.

We could not understand why she needed to do this, and when asked she always had a good explanation: The dresses were either too big or too small. If too big, her reason for taking them apart was to make a new style or to make them fit better. If too small, she took them apart to make them into something else, maybe just a top or a skirt. This way the dresses could be salvaged and used constructively.

Once the clothes were taken apart, they never quite got back to their original form and were eventually discarded, because keeping them caused too much clutter. She had so many things in her room competing for space.

All the walls and windows were still covered, no matter what time of year. Pieces of fabric and clothing were all over the sewing machine, the chest of drawers, in the closet, in the sewing basket, on the floor . . . it was a mess! The one exception to this was her bed, which always looked as if it belonged to a military officer. There were no creases in sight, pillows were fluffed to the max, sheets tucked in and folded at the corners, and bedspreads folded neatly at the foot of the bed. The bed was an oasis in the middle of chaotic madness.

I had to replace her entire wardrobe every three to four months, not because she had no clothes but because the clothes she had were now in a hundred pieces all over her room. To save some money, I began shopping at the secondhand store. If the secondhand store was having a sale, I would purchase a lot of clothing and only give her a few pieces at a time because it was obvious to all of us what would happen to them. Once she destroyed the clothing, I would give her some additional pieces. The destruction of her clothing became a permanent habit.

MY YOUNGER SISTER, SALLY

Mom was always the head of the household, and we lived by her rules. She would always say, "I work, so I make the rules. When you get a job and begin to contribute, I will consider your input." When I got older and was helping out a little financially, I had ideas of my own and wanted to introduce some of them to the household. Mom would have none of it. She and I butted heads a lot prior to my leaving for college. I was stubborn, but she put her foot down; it was her way or the highway.

As I tried to become more independent, Mom and Sally grew even closer. I moved from Brooklyn to Boston in 1982 to attend college, leaving Sally and Mom in the apartment we had lived in for many years. Several years after I left for college, Sally got married and moved only two blocks away. Mom was a constant presence in Sally's life. I became envious of their relationship. They knew everything about one another. Being on the independent side, I did not confide too much of my personal life to Mom. If I got myself into any type of trouble, I would work it out myself, because Mom always had too much on her plate and I never wanted to add any stress to her life.

When Sally had her first baby, she and her husband ran into some financial difficulties and they moved into the same building with Mom, eventually having to give up their apartment and live with her. I think Mom enjoyed that more than anything else.

After graduating from college, I took a year off and then began looking for work in Boston. I was unsuccessful in finding a job in my field, and moved back to Brooklyn at the end of 1988. I moved in with Sally and her husband for approximately six months. By this time Mom had moved to Washington, DC, to assist my older sister, Amy, with her children. I was much older then and realized that my independence was not such a

58

big deal. By that time, my relationship with Mom had gotten a lot better. As the old folks say, "Age brings reason." I became a more reasonable and understanding person once I lived away from home. Being away from Mom made me realize what she had to do in order to keep the family on the right path.

Sally and Mom had become so close they spoke on a daily basis. When Sally had to make major decisions in her life, she always consulted Mom.

Fast-forward to 2011: The once great relationship had deteriorated into a daily conflict. Mom and Sally would get into intense confrontations over fairly minor issues; Mom's default manner of speech now was to scream at anyone who she felt was bothering her.

Mom began complaining to anyone who would listen that Sally was hiding things from her and speaking badly about her when she was not around. Additionally, she claimed Sally had changed and was not the same loving child she used to be. When asked to explain how Sally had changed, Mom simply would say, "Well, she just changed."

I felt really bad for both of them. Mom had become so mean. It did not matter what was said to her; she took everything as a slight. Sally had to be so careful about everything she said. It got so bad that they hardly communicated. If Sally needed to speak with Mom and called out to her, Mom would pretend she did not hear her.

The living conditions in the house became unbearable. Mom refused to speak to Sally and angrily refused to listen to any reason. We tried telling Mom that everyone was the same and nothing had changed. But she was convinced Sally was plotting against her. She told me she heard Sally whispering things to people on the phone, and she knew there were plans to do her harm. When Mom went to church, she told people at church how horribly she was being treated at home. We did not understand why she was doing this, but she believed everything she said.

Mom relayed a story to me regarding something Sally had told her. According to Mom, Sally said if her father was from

59

another ethnic background, she would have hated Mom for that. This story kept coming up in most of the conversations we had. I finally asked Sally if it was true, and she said it was. However, she had told Mom this when she was a rebellious thirteen-year-old girl. Mom repeated the story as though it had happened recently.

One day Mom called me and confessed that she hated Sally. When I asked her why, she claimed Sally hated her first; therefore, she felt justified in hating her. She began telling her few friends and acquaintances in the neighborhood how horrible Sally was. She would say she was selfish and that she bought expensive things for herself and Tara, and only brought home rags for her.

The church we attend is a very diverse church comprised of members from many different parts of the world. The elders of the church decided to have an International Day and requested that everyone dress in their native outfit symbolizing the culture in which they were born. Sally went out and bought dresses for everyone. She and Tara dressed alike, and she bought a different outfit for Mom. When Mom saw the outfit she got so angry, she threw it at Sally. Mom called me crying, saying she could not understand why Sally had become so mean. "The outfit is ugly and cheap. I will not be wearing it," she said. No matter how much I reasoned with her, it was no use.

The International Day came and we all dressed in our native clothes, but Mom wore a regular dress. At church, when she was asked why she was not in a native outfit, she made a very mean comment about how she was not appreciated by her horrible child and how the dress that was given to her was awful so she had no choice but to come in her everyday clothes.

At home, the house was now either very quiet or extremely loud, depending on Mom's mood. It became like a war zone. There was always a problem, and each time I spoke to Mom, she told me in a loud voice how much she hated Sally. Under her breath she would call her a bitch.

Because I could not get to the bottom of what was bothering Mom, I asked a mutual friend who visited on a regular basis to come by one Sunday. When she arrived at the house I was already there, but we had to beg Mom to come downstairs. Mom sat on the far side of the room, away from Sally. We told her we were trying to find out what was wrong between her and Sally. Mom started screaming, "I hate her! I want her out of my sight! She is the worst person I know!" As she screamed she began to cry.

Sally was also crying, saying she had done nothing to Mom. Mom got even angrier and screamed, "You are a bold-faced liar. You know what you have done." I had to ask Sally to leave in order to calm Mom down. What was going on?

SEEING THE UNSEEN

As Mom's disease progressed, she began complaining about her eyesight. She repeatedly took off her glasses and rubbed her eyes. I assumed she needed new glasses. One Saturday when she visited me, she told me she was seeing horizontal lines in her eyes. She described in detail how the lines kept opening and closing; she said it was similar to when she opened and closed the window shades. I was not sure what was happening to her and tried to assure her that perhaps new glasses would solve the problem.

I made an appointment for her with her eye doctor and got a prescription for new glasses, but the new glasses did not make the horizontal lines go away. Unfortunately, she kept telling me the lines were there, and she began seeing them more and more as the weeks went by.

In retrospect, I assume her brain cells were being attacked by the disease and the lines she saw were side effects of the disease.

LEAVING

The year 2010 was very difficult for everyone. As the year dragged on, fights were a regular occurrence. Mom was always slamming the doors, and the everyday chaos of living became overwhelming at the house. Mom's behavior became more unpredictable with each passing day. One moment she would be in a great mood, and then the next she would be screaming at someone for no apparent reason. Everyone had to be so careful around her; even if someone said something nice to her, she might take it as an attack. The crying was endless. Sally would call me crying; then Mom would call crying. It was so bad I thought I would lose my mind. I was getting stories from both sides, and God forbid if I gave my opinion, especially to Mom. So I just listened and sank into a state of gloom. What was happening to Mom? The doctor kept saying there was no problem, yet she had become this impossible monster.

Mom began watching some daytime talk shows and would cry for hours over some of that drivel. There was always something or someone that would trigger her crying. I am not sure if she always knew why she was crying, but cry she did. As far as she was concerned, the entire world was against her.

One day while we were driving to church, I asked Mom a simple question. It was so simple that I can't even recall what it was. Once the question left my lips, she started screaming at me. When I tried to calm her down, she insisted I had it in for her, that I had wanted to tell her off for some time, I was siding with everyone against her, we all wanted her dead, and we were doing our best to kill her. When I said I had no idea what she was talking about, the screaming simply intensified. She was shouting so loudly that I got a headache.

Tara, who was sitting on the backseat next to Mom, tried to say something. Mom screamed at her, "I will slap your face off if you don't shut your lips." Here I was driving on the highway and Mom was threatening my niece! I was afraid because I knew she was capable of doing exactly what she had said. I raised my voice louder than hers and told her to stop the screaming and threats instantly. I guess I must have jarred her back to reality because, to my surprise, she stopped. She just glared at me from the backseat. She was crying, as usual, and then she looked out the window. She refused to speak for the rest of the ride. I was thankful she said nothing more. Once we arrived at church, the cherub emerged in her.

After church we went to my house for lunch, which she ate in silence. After lunch I asked her if she could please tell me what was going on. She moved away from the table, screaming at me to leave her alone. She went to the living room and I followed, repeating the same question as her same responses simply got louder and louder. At that time I was really trying to understand what was going on with her. We all knew something was wrong, but none of us knew what it was. There was no logical explanation as to why her behavior had changed so much.

I finally walked away, not knowing what else to do. As I did, she again told me to leave her alone. I felt so helpless that I could do nothing for her, and each day she seemed to slip further and further into this dark, aggressive place. Mom was now becoming a stranger to us!

THE TRIP

In the fall of 2010, Mom's behavior became so erratic, and the frequency of her threats against Sally and Tara increased to such a frenzied pace, that I began to have visions of her making good on them. She was angry almost all the time now. She would actually get in your face as though she was about to do whatever she said she was going to do—rip your face off, punch you, kick your ass, kill you; you name it and she was willing to do it. Most of the time, we would slowly back away from her, but I think she put the fear of God in Sally.

Her hatred for Sally seemed to have grown to a sinister level, causing me to be gravely concerned for Sally's safety. I really felt that, given the right opportunity and incentive, she was capable of killing her. The house they lived in has three bedrooms on the second floor and one on the first floor. After moving in, Mom had converted the three-season porch into a bedroom and Sally occupied the bedroom on the first floor. I began to have visions of Mom coming down the stairs in the middle of the night and stabbing Sally to death. This vision became so vivid that I began to think it would happen any day. I told Sally to be very careful and to lock the door at night when she went to sleep. The fear was not irrational, given the way Mom spoke about Sally and her hatred toward her.

Mom began asking me to send her to see her sister and brothers who lived in the Caribbean. It was a relief when she made the request. I felt elated that she wanted to go away. I quickly purchased a nonrefundable one-way plane ticket for her. I thought we would have some relief from her mood swings and terrible outbursts.

Our family in the Caribbean knew we were having lots of problems with her, but everyone agreed the tropical climate might be good for her. The initial plan was that she would stay in the city with her youngest sister, Aunt Deloris. When my aunt became overwhelmed, Mom would go to the country to be with her brother Ben.

With everything set for the trip, we awaited the departure date. A week before Mom was set to leave, I reminded her about her flight. "What flight?" she asked. I reminded her about the ticket I had purchased at her request, but she replied, "I don't know what you are talking about. I never asked you to do anything. If you think you can get rid of me that easily, you better think again. This is my house and I am not going anywhere. No one is going to take this away from me, and if you think you can, you have a rude awakening waiting for you."

I dropped the subject because I did not want to upset her more. The day of her departure came and went, and she did not budge an inch; no matter what we said, she refused to go to the airport. The ticket was now worthless. I was angry with her. I could hardly bring myself to talk to her for a couple of days. She was clueless as to why I was so upset.

A month later she again began asking about going to visit her family. When I reminded her that I had purchased a ticket for her less than a month before, she quickly chided me that it was not nice to lie. She said I was not being nice by trying to make her believe something that never happened. She gave me one of those looks that had become commonplace with her now; she would slightly turn her head and look at me out of the corner of her eye in a mischievous way. She had completely forgotten about the previous ticket.

I was annoyed about the money I had lost from the first ticket and promised myself that I wouldn't buy another ticket, but she kept asking to go. Finally, I gave in and purchased a second ticket. My husband was patient, even though this could have been another complete waste of money. In any event, seeing how her memory was getting progressively worse, we decided to book her on a midnight flight to go home. We made the arrangements and the flight was booked for midnight on December 25. We assumed this would be the best thing because she would be able to sleep on the flight, and the following morning she would be at her destination.

The entire family had breakfast at my home Christmas morning. After breakfast, we opened gifts. Christmas is my favorite time of the year, and I always go overboard with the gift giving. We had such a wonderful morning.

Prior to the day's activities, I had asked Mom if she was packed. She responded, "Of course I am packed." After breakfast, I wished her a good trip and promised to call her on a weekly basis. I was unsure when I would see her again. I had once again purchased a one-way ticket because I was not sure how long she would be staying.

To be honest, I was relieved she was going. It had been such a terrible year, and everyone's nerves were beyond frazzled. It was so difficult dealing with Mom and her constant changes in behavior. She had become verbally abusive and had turned into this horrible person; just the thought of her leaving made me happy. In my heart, I was hoping she would love being back home so much she would not want to return.

Mom was in a great mood Christmas morning, and it was truly good to see her this way. Just before noon, my family headed back to their house and my husband and I went to his parents' home for a late lunch and gift exchange. The afternoon progressed well. We eventually decided to return home around 9:30 Christmas night. As we got in the car, I glanced at my watch and told Stephen, "I guess Mom must be at the airport now." It was an international flight, so she would need several hours for predeparture check-in.

I was concerned about Mom's safety on the flight and asked Sally to seek permission from the airline to have someone assist her with her boarding and deplaning.

On the return trip home, traffic was unusually light and we made it home within an hour. As we pulled into the driveway, we saw Sally's van parked with the engine running. I remarked how strange it was that they were back at our house. As soon as we parked, Sally came out of the van and approached our car crying. She said Mom had refused to exit the van when they got to the airport. She told us she was tired of Mom's behavior and she was not going to take her back to the house because she could no longer live in the same house with her.

On the way back from the airport, Mom once again became verbally abusive to Sally, but this time it was worse than ever. Sally's fiancé had driven them to the airport. Mom proceeded to curse Sally, telling her what a whore she was. In Mom's mind, Sally courted many men and she wanted it known that she was a "bad" girl with a terrible reputation. Mom told her she was never wanted as a baby and it would have been far better if she had aborted her rather than carried her to full term. The entire ugly scene was recorded by Sally's fiancé. While Mom was shouting and cursing her, she was also beating the headrest with her fist trying to hit Sally! The screaming was still going on when we arrived home.

I got out of my car and could hear Mom in the van yelling. The entire thing sounded just awful. Two days later I was shown the recording Sally's fiancé had made. It was even worse than what Sally had described; the language that Mom used was terrible, and the names she called Sally were just unbelievable.

Stephen exited our car and went over to the van and opened the rear door, where Mom was sitting as though nothing had happened. I was next to Stephen, and he asked her why she was not at the airport. "I don't have to be there. Sally is attempting to get rid of me, and no one told me I was going anywhere until I arrived at the airport." Once again I found myself furious with Mom. Why was she acting this way? I told her we were going back to the airport and told Sally to go into our house. Stephen and I got into the van with Sally's fiancé still at the wheel and headed out of the driveway.

Mom was crying, telling me no one loved her and we were trying to get rid of her. She had no one whom she could depend on and everyone hated her. As proof, we were now sending her away without her permission. How could we do this to her? She sounded so helpless, but I did not feel sorry for her because I was just too angry.

The airport drive took twelve minutes. Normally it is a longer drive, but we were breaking all the speed limits to get her back to the airport in time to get her on the plane. Once we arrived, we got out of the van and basically dragged her inside to get checked in. She just kept looking at me, and all of a sudden she seemed so lost. I told Stephen I was not sure her suitcase would make the flight because we were running really late. We attempted to get a pass to accompany her to the gate, but the office was closed and we had very little time left to check her in.

Once we got on line, there was only one other person in line just ahead of us, a young mother with her baby. I was so afraid Mom would get lost trying to find her way to the gate that I touched the young lady on her shoulder and asked what flight she was taking. To my relief she told me she and Mom were on the same flight. I explained to her that Mom was somewhat forgetful and asked if she could please help her to the gate because I did not want her getting lost. I guess she heard the desperation in my voice and readily agreed to assist Mom.

Because of their lateness, a little mobile vehicle came for them to get both passengers to the gate in a hurry. The driver honked the horn and they got on. Once they climbed on, Mom sat facing me and waved good-bye as the little vehicle disappeared out of sight. As I lost sight of her, I wondered how she would make it off the flight. I was so concerned that once the plane arrived at its final destination she would not know which way to go or what to do. I was positive she would be unable to navigate her way to find her baggage and get through customs.

My fear for Mom was constant because she had become so forgetful and volatile. It was like watching a beautiful flower slowly wilt away before your eyes, all the while knowing there was nothing anyone could do to stop the wilting.

The following day when I spoke to Aunt Deloris, I learned everything went okay. The young lady with the baby helped Mom off the airplane, helped her find her luggage, and even stayed with her until my cousins arrived to pick her up. I was grateful for the kindness of this total stranger.

I spoke with Mom and she sounded so good. She said she was very happy to be home and my aunt was being nice to her. Long gone was the memory of the previous night with all its drama, threats, and tears; she was once again with her family and was happy, or so it seemed.

I promised to call again in a couple of days to check on her. I said the coming New Year would be great and we would have a happy New Year. As I spoke the words about happiness, I guess I was trying to convince myself it would get better for all of us, but someplace deep inside my head I knew my words were not true; I was just hoping they could be. I was wishing we could go back to the old days when she used to be nice, kind, and good, but I knew those days were gone forever.

FAMILY VISIT

While Mom was away, I called her weekly to get a progress report on how things were going. She stayed with my aunt for two weeks; then she began nagging her about going to see her brother. Initially my aunt did not want her to go, but finally she agreed to send her to the country. Once she was in the country things were fine for a few days, but then the problems began.

I was told she would wake up early in the morning and make a huge breakfast for four people. She then proceeded to wake everyone up so they could eat. My uncle's son, wife, and young child lived in the house. Mom would wake the baby up, give him a bath, comb his hair, and dress him for the day's activities. Her old habit of washing every day continued—however, with a small twist. My uncle did not own a washing machine, so she began washing her clothes by hand. Then she hung the clothes to dry on the line that was outside of the house, and retrieved the clothes from the line in less than an hour. She would then neatly fold up the clothes and place them in a bag or her suitcase, even though they were still very wet. When she was told the clothes were wet, she would argue they were completely dry. No one could make her hang them up to dry.

In the general vicinity where Ben lives, Mom had another brother living within easy walking distance. Each day she took the baby with her and walked the half mile to visit him, but she quickly began forgetting how to get back to Ben's home. She would wander aimlessly trying to find her way back. It was one long country road with no other streets running parallel to the one she took; however, by this time she was so confused she forgot how to navigate this one street.

Her now famous temper began kicking in. She now saw the farmer on a daily basis, the one who she was convinced had blocked her ability to get the land she wanted to purchase. He lived across the way from Ben, and seeing him inflamed her anger.

When Ben attempted to reason with her, he also ended up on the receiving end of her wrath. She began accusing him of turning against her. She began fighting with him on a daily basis. One day she decided to stop speaking to him entirely. On this particular day she cooked a huge meal that included a fish dish, but instead of leaving it for the family, she fed the fish to the dog. Her stay in the country lasted all of two weeks before Ben called Aunt Deloris and informed her Mom would be coming back to her.

I fully understood why he returned her to Aunt Deloris. He could not control her, and I believe he was somewhat intimidated by his older sister. I had witnessed Mom's aggression. I knew how hurtful her language could get when she did not get her way. I also knew she could intimidate anyone. I was very careful to stay out of her way when she flew into her rages and could imagine how my uncle must have felt. It was not easy dealing with her. I am sure she got in his face with her horrible attitude, and he may have assumed she was going to attack him.

Ben could not stop Mom from leaving the house. He could not prevent her from cooking banquet-size meals. He could not stop her from washing clothes and folding them up while they were still wet. In just two weeks, she had completely worn him down.

Once she returned to Aunt Deloris, she kept asking to go back to Ben, but he always had an excuse why she could not visit. I felt really bad for him because I knew he wanted her to visit. But unfortunately, her threatening and uncharacteristic behavior was too unnerving for him. I am her child, and I too had to send her away because I was no longer capable of handling her.

A few weeks after returning to Aunt Deloris, Uncle Ben and a distant cousin visited Mom. Once they arrived, Mom mysteriously disappeared. When everyone in the house discovered her disappearance, they began looking for her in each room, but she was not there. They finally went outside and found her, suitcase in hand, sitting in the backseat of the car that was parked in front of Aunt Deloris's house. Someone asked her, "Where are you going?" She responded, "To visit my brother." It took them several hours to talk her out of the car.

After this, Ben began calling on the phone to check up on Mom rather than visit. He did not want to upset her, and no one wanted a repeat of her standoff in the car.

Thereafter, she always kept her overnight bag and suitcase packed and on the porch, just in case she needed to leave in a hurry. Her clothing in the suitcase was still wet, and the washing continued.

At night when Mom went to sleep, my aunt would take the wet clothes out of the suitcase and hang them up to dry. If my aunt forgot to take the clothes out, the following morning she would take the smelly clothes out of the suitcase and wash them again.

Mom always maintained a garden no matter where she lived. While she was staying with Aunt Deloris, she was always outside in the garden. The house was fenced in with a huge front gate. The cement wall that surrounded the house was at least ten feet tall.

Each day Mom woke up early, got dressed in some of her damp clothing, and went into the garden while talking to Aunt Deloris's three dogs.

Once Aunt Deloris woke up, they had breakfast and Mom would go back outside. Sometimes Aunt Deloris would go outside with Mom, but if by chance Aunt Deloris needed something in the house and asked Mom to retrieve it, that would be a problem. It took Mom less than one minute to get to the stairs, but in that time she would have forgotten what she was going to get. She would call out, asking for a reminder of what Aunt Deloris needed. Once inside the house, she would have to be reminded again and again what she needed to get. Her retention level was rapidly dwindling.

Uncharacteristically, she began stealing food. Aunt Deloris was forced to hide food from her. When meals were prepared, Mom's portion was dished out for her. If not, once everyone was out of sight Mom would take more food and eat it. Nothing could be left on the kitchen counter because if it was, Mom would eat all of it.

Her obsession with cooking continued. Each day she wanted to cook several meals. Aunt Deloris feared Mom might burn herself on the stove and tried very hard to keep her out of the kitchen. Aunt Deloris began complaining to me when I called about all the things Mom was doing. She could not get her to listen to anything she told her.

After a couple of months with Aunt Deloris, when I called and asked to speak to Mom, we no longer had a normal conversation. Mom would begin whispering on the phone, telling me she no longer trusted my aunt and everyone was treating her badly. Her paranoia had come back, to my dismay. I knew no one was treating her badly; it was all in her head.

Several months after Mom went to the Caribbean, I got a phone call from Sally, who had just gotten off the phone with Aunt Deloris—who had told her that earlier that day, Mom had run away!

On this particular Wednesday around 11:30, Mom came through the bedroom that was just off the kitchen and quickly looked through the doorway. Aunt Deloris was preparing lunch and did not look directly at Mom. When Mom saw this, she went back into the room and disappeared. After lunch was made, Aunt Deloris called out to Mom but got no response. She searched each room, but Mom was nowhere to be found. She even checked outside with no luck. My cousin lives in the apartment on the first floor of the house. My aunt thought maybe the door was unlocked and Mom had entered the apartment. She went downstairs and searched, but Mom was gone. My aunt panicked, and then she looked at the front gate and saw it slightly opened. She was now frantic because she realized Mom had left the property.

Aunt Deloris called her daughter at work and told her Mom was missing. Her daughter in turn called a few friends, and several cars began a search for Mom. It now had been approximately two hours since my aunt had last seen Mom.

Mom was unfamiliar with the area where my aunt lived, and that made the situation worse. Three separate cars began sweeping the neighborhood street by street in search of Mom. As the hours dragged by, my aunt began to wonder if someone had seen Mom leave the property and picked her up in his or her car. She began to fear the worst.

Five hours and many miles later, the search was still on. My cousin and her friend kept going from street to street. They were about to turn down yet another street when her friend said, "Do not turn. Let's go straight on this street." Several minutes later they spotted Mom on the opposite side of the street, not far from the local highway. She had her pocketbook and was walking briskly.

My cousin and her friend broke a few traffic laws and quickly made a U-turn, pulling up alongside Mom and calling out to her. Mom said a hardy hello and continued her brisk walk. They had to park on the side of the road and follow her on foot. When they caught up to her, she said she was going to visit her brother's house, but she had made a wrong turn and was now attempting to get back to the street where he lived. They offered to take her to his home, but she refused, insisting she would find the house on her own. With the traffic going by, they kept begging her to come with them. It took them more than ten minutes to talk her into getting in the car.

When she finally got in the car, she was annoyed. She could not understand what the fuss was about. She had no clue she had been missing for such a long time and she had made everyone extremely worried.

When she got back to the house, they asked how she had gotten as far as she had. She said she had walked to the street corner and two young ladies hailed a cab. She got into the cab, and when the young ladies got out of the cab farther downtown, she paid for the ride and got out of the car. She then began the search for her brother's house. Apparently, she searched several streets but failed to find the house. She then turned down another street and was still searching for his house when she was found.

When I spoke to Mom a day after the incident, she could not understand why it was such a big deal that she had gone looking for her brother. I do not believe she remembered exactly what had happened because she quickly changed the subject. She informed me she no longer wanted to stay with Aunt Deloris because she was sure she was plotting something sinister against her and something terrible was going to happen to her very soon. When I asked her what she meant by sinister, she was unable to tell me what the plans were, but she did assure me she would remember the next time we spoke to one another. The relationship between the siblings had deteriorated just the way it had with her children. Aunt Deloris was very close to Mom, but as far as Mom was concerned, the relationship was over.

Prior to Mom's taxi adventure, I sent money to Aunt Deloris to assist in Mom's care. I always made sure Mom got money to purchase what she wanted. I wanted her to have her independence and did not want her to beg anyone for money. After the incident, I gave specific instructions that Mom was not to be given any money at all. Having money and access to cabs made getting lost too easy for her. I feared if she ran away a second time we would not be as fortunate and perhaps she would never be found. Why tempt fate?

For the first time in her adult life, Mom was not allowed to have money. Each time we spoke, she asked for some pocket change, as she put it, because she was broke. I would lie and say I would send her money, knowing full well I was never sending her money again.

MELTDOWN

It had been five months since Mom went to visit Aunt Deloris. With each phone call I was told how difficult it had become to take care of her.

To make matters worse, Mom would not listen to anyone. She did exactly what she wanted, when she wanted, and how she wanted. The frustrating routine repeated itself on a daily basis: her clothes were folded and packed away while still wet, and what did not go in the suitcase was spread all over the house. When Aunt Deloris tried to speak to her about it, Mom yelled at her. Her stealing continued; anything she found would be hidden away under the bed, in the pillowcases, in the closet, or in people's shoes—wherever she found a spot, she would hide whatever she stole. Stolen perishable items began to rot where she left them.

Mom began rearranging the rooms in the house. Nothing was left unmoved. She now began repeating herself and would ask the same question over and over again.

It was becoming too much for my aunt to handle. Mom began telling me they were stealing her money. She now conducted all our conversations in a whisper. She told me her conversations were being taped or someone was listening in on what she was saying. She also began telling me how she and Aunt Deloris hated one another.

Mom referred to Aunt Deloris as the "skinny mean bitch," and she began crying every time we spoke. I was hoping the crying had gone away, but it was back and now she said she wanted to come back to the United States.

I began to worry more about Aunt Deloris because she was always on the sickly side and the conversations about Mom's behavior were becoming dire. She constantly repeated how hard it was to care for Mom. I knew she was telling the truth. We had sent Mom to her because we could no longer care for her. Mom had become so confrontational and stubborn with her that I was afraid for Aunt Deloris's safety.

Six months after Mom went to visit her family, I began making arrangements for her return. The thought of her return put me in such a funk that I could not sleep for several days.

I couldn't allow Mom to travel alone because I knew it would be impossible for her to find her way through customs and out of the airport. I also knew I had to find another place for her to live because she could no longer live with Sally. I could not live with her either. I was out of the house all day and she could not be trusted to be alone.

We contacted several assisted-living facilities, and my husband and I visited a few in the surrounding neighborhoods close to our home. The visits to these facilities were depressing. We were careful to explain exactly what was going on with Mom, and we were assured there was a "lockdown floor" where she would be safe and unable to escape. It sounded like a good idea; however, once we were told the cost, I knew we could not afford it. The lowest annual price was $133,000.

I called Amy, who lives in California, to let her know I had to bring Mom back because of her behavior. I also informed her we were looking into assisted-living care for her. Amy insisted Mom could not live in a nursing home and she would care for her. I told her she had not seen Mom in some time and Mom's behavior was extremely bad. I honestly told her she could not handle Mom. Amy insisted she would be able to do it.

Arrangements were made for Mom's return. Sally and her family would visit Aunt Deloris, and when they came back to the United States, Mom would come back with them.

I had to send new clothing for the trip because her current wardrobe was ruined. If they did not smell, the rest were in ruins because when she found a pair of scissors she just cut whatever she laid her hands on.

When the family arrived, Mom was pleased to see Tara, Cindy, and my brother-in-law, but the goodwill did not extend to Sally. During the six-plus months Mom hadn't seen Sally, it seemed her hatred toward her simply grew rather than subsided. Mom immediately began referring to Sally as "the dry-legged bitch."

Mom now had two people to hate, Sally and Aunt Deloris. The complaints kept coming, even though I told her she would be returning to the United Sates. I told her she would be living with Amy in sunny California. I was trying to convince myself that once she was somewhere else, she would be happy.

The weekend before Mom was due to return; I called her and reminded her to be nice to Aunt Deloris and not to forget to thank her for letting her stay with her. Mom was insistent she was not going to thank "the bitch." She said she was glad to leave, and she was never going back there for a visit.

In an ironic twist, she was right about never going back to visit. About a year after Mom's return, Aunt Deloris died from liver cancer. Prior to Mom's return, Aunt Deloris kept telling me about a pain she had in her belly. Previously she had gallstones, so the doctor assumed it was gallstones and planned to remove them. In late May 2012, a test revealed a mass on her liver and she was diagnosed with liver cancer. I asked Deloris's children not to tell her about the cancer, but I was overruled. Once she was told, she just got into bed, and seven weeks after the diagnosis she was dead. To this day, Mom has no knowledge of her death.

In my heart I know Mom did not contribute to Aunt Deloris's illness, but I know she gave her a hard time. None of us knew how ill she was at the time. After she died, I felt really guilty that I had taken my problem and dumped it on her.

THE RETURN

Amy came from California a week prior to Mom's return. I was a bit apprehensive about letting Mom live with her because Amy is very emotional and I knew she could not handle Mom in her present state. However, with limited options I had no choice but to allow Mom to move to California. Desperate people always do desperate things, and looking back, I should have known better.

The day of Mom's flight, I called to be sure everything was in order. Mom sounded excited when I said she was coming home. I told her I looked forward to seeing her the next morning; she said she was also looking forward to seeing me.

I spoke to Aunt Deloris, who was relieved Mom was leaving. The past seven months had taken a toll on her. The stress of having to be constantly vigilant with Mom for all those months had made her more anxious than she normally was.

Now that Mom was leaving, Aunt Deloris began telling me a few stories about what had happened while she was there. When Mom went to church, she would kiss everyone over and over again. Some people at the church knew Mom was ill, but others did not. One young man got so flustered by Mom's kissing habit that whenever he saw her he would go the other way. She also related another story about Mom visiting her in-law's family; it seemed Mom was flirting with her in-law's husband. His wife was sitting in the living room, and Mom just kept saying things to the man, winking at him, trying to cuddle up to him, touching him, and making off-color jokes. My aunt was beyond embarrassed. Naturally, Mom had no recollection of these incidents.

Mom also began showing an interest in any young man she saw; she wanted to go out with all of them and did her best to get their attention.

I felt terrible for Aunt Deloris and truly sorry for Mom.

THE JOURNEY BACK

Mom and the rest of the family were booked on a midnight flight back to New Jersey. Once again, we decided the midnight flight back would have a more calming effect on her. She could sleep and that would be good for her—and less stressful for everyone else. I knew she would have no trouble falling asleep because she was, and still is, a great sleeper. We used to say Mom could fall asleep on the edge of a pin; you would be talking to her and in nothing flat she would fall asleep and begin talking in her sleep.

When we were younger, we would be having a conversation with Mom and she would fall asleep midsentence. I always assumed it was because she had a couple of jobs and was always tired. I later learned she had always fallen asleep at the drop of a hat, even when she was much younger.

My family had developed a bad habit of missing flights, and because Mom would be accompanying Amy to Los Angeles, I wanted to make doubly sure they made the flight. I made sure Sally reconfirmed the flight. She assured me she had done so; all was fine and their arrival would be as planned. Amy had booked a nonrefundable ticket for her trip to New Jersey and had already said she would return to Los Angeles "with or without Mom."

The night arrived. I was a bit anxious because the flight would be landing at 5:30 the following morning and I had to be sure we were at the airport on time, just in case Mom had behaved badly on the flight or had a fight with Sally.

Stephen and I settled in for the short night of rest. At around 10:30, the phone rang; it was Sally. She began the conversation by saying they were at the airport, but there was a problem. I heard the word "problem" and panicked. I recall feeling very sick as soon as I heard there was a problem with the flight. Sally had misread the flight manifest. They had been booked on the previous night's flight. The flight they thought they were supposed to be on was sold out, so they were on standby.

I was now in full panic mode. I reminded her Mom could not be on the flight alone; she had to have someone on the flight with her. I told her she had to explain Mom's condition to the boarding attendant so they could have first consideration if there was a cancellation or someone did not show up for the flight.

At 12:30 Sally called again. There was only one seat available on the plane and it was given to Mom. During the first conversation, I had become sick; now I felt even sicker and was truly scared for Mom's life. There was no way she would be able to get through the airport alone, and even if she did somehow, she would be unable to find us. The airport is huge with lots of gates, and in Mom's fragile state of mind she would have no idea what to do or where to go.

A few months prior, at a nearby airport, a Westminster purebred dog was shipped in for a competition. Somehow the dog got out of his carrying cage, made his way through an open door, ran into the nearby marshes, and was never seen again. I had visions of Mom opening the wrong door and wandering out into the marshes.

Sally assured me she had explained to the check-in desk that Mom had memory problems and that they had made arrangements for someone to accompany her when she disembarked. This brought me no comfort because I knew special arrangements were usually made in advance of flight departures. There was nothing I could do now but hope and pray she would be all right.

I did not sleep the entire night. We left the house at 5:40 and arrived at the airport promptly at 6:00. We checked the arrival board and saw the flight had landed. Once we saw this, we proceeded directly to the arrival area and waited. The minutes slowly ticked by. While standing there, I was trying to picture in my mind how Mom would get through customs and find her luggage. The question that I did not have an answer for was whether she would be able to find us.

We waited as close to the exit as possible. It was crowded with people from all over the world exiting through the gates. The minutes turned into an hour, then two hours. I was so nervous that every muscle in my body ached. I felt if I moved my skin would just fall off my bones. I just stood without moving and kept my eyes on the exit door. I kept thinking she was lost and that if she was indeed lost, she would not realize it.

Whenever I saw a wheelchair, my hopes would be lifted only to be dashed. Finally, after two and a half hours, she emerged pulling two suitcases. She was looking around and I began to frantically wave at her. She finally saw us and began calling to us, signaling us to come over to her. I kept waving her forward because we were not authorized to enter this secured section of the airport. She kept calling me and I kept waving her forward. She finally came toward us and we greeted her with a hug.

She began telling me that one of the suitcases she was pulling was not hers, but some lady had made her take it. She went on to say she thought she was going crazy because she could not recall very much, and then the familiar crying started. I reassured her she was not crazy and told her she was going to be all right. As the years have passed, I've learned how to lie to Mom about her health; I knew she was not going to be all right. As a matter of fact, for as long as she lived, she was never going to be all right again.

We took the suitcases and headed toward the parking lot with Mom in tow, crying. She kept repeating that one of the suitcases had been given to her in error.

When we arrived at the parking lot and found the car, I told Mom to please sit in the backseat and asked Stephen to put both suitcases in the trunk, just to get them out of her sight. She sat in the backseat, still trying to figure out what had happened and talking about the suitcase. I sat in the front seat and Stephen drove the car. Mom kept talking and I sat quietly and wept all the way home. I had never been so scared in all my life. I had visions of Mom being lost and never being able to exit the airport. I was not sure who the woman was who had assisted her with her suitcase. No one from the airline assisted her because the request for assistance had come too late.

My crying was a combination of many things: I wept because she was so lost. I wept for myself because of my helplessness in assisting her. She had always been such an independent person, coming and going as she pleased, traveling for years by herself, and now here she was unable to navigate getting out of an airport. I also wept because I knew she had no future—that in the weeks, months, and years to come she would only get sicker and no one would be able to do anything to help her. But deep down, I guess I was also weeping for myself because I was scared. I do not have a crystal ball and I am unable to see what the future holds. That is the hardest part of this disease. Frankly speaking, I do not want to end up like my mother.

A SHORT REST

We arrived at our house twenty minutes after leaving the airport. Stephen and Mom had breakfast. I was unable to eat because of the stress of the last several hours.

After breakfast Mom said she was tired. I took her upstairs and put her to bed; she fell asleep before I left the room. I was happy she still slept very well. At least when she was asleep she was not afraid and did not have to worry about not remembering things.

I looked at her sleeping and felt so sorry for her because she had no control over what was happening to her and we could not help her. Without her permission, this disease had taken up residence in her head and was slowly, but surely, sucking the very life out of her brain.

I returned downstairs and we took her suitcases out of the trunk. Upon opening the suitcases, I discovered most of her clothing was damp or wet. Some of it smelled bad. I took the clothes out and quickly washed and dried them. I could not fully get the smell out of some of the clothes, even after washing, so I put them in the garbage. I was also forced to leave the suitcases open to air out. Whatever was left I packed into one suitcase, making sure to hide the suitcase that Mom believed was not hers.

Her flight to Los Angeles was in a few hours. She was confused enough, and I did not wish to add to her confusion by giving her the suitcase she insisted was not hers.

She woke up a few hours later. I told her she was going back to the airport to go to California. She did not acknowledge what I told her. I was not sure if she had not heard me or if she had decided just to ignore me.

She began a conversation with Stephen and kept asking him the same questions every couple of minutes. I just sat and looked at her, wondering what was actually going on in her head. I knew she was not remembering, but I did not know if she knew and understood she was forgetting.

CALIFORNIA, HERE WE COME

I was not very anxious regarding the flight to Los Angeles because I knew Mom had Amy with her. When I spoke with Amy later on that day, she told me the flight to LA was uneventful and Mom slept most of the way there.

Upon arriving at Amy's house, Mom unpacked, took several showers, and then got dressed. Amy said she saw Mom put on three panties, two bras, and three dresses. Amy was very upset and, true to form, her fussing with Mom began on the first day. No matter how many times we reminded Amy about Mom's failing memory, she still tried to reason with her. Somehow we could not get her to understand that it did not matter to Mom who said what because as soon as it was said, it just went directly out of her brain.

In the days after their arrival I got a daily update on what was going on. Mom wanted to cook, or she was outside digging and planting, was not listening, was wearing too much clothing, and on and on it went. I kept telling Amy to leave Mom alone, just let her do whatever she wanted to do as long as she was not in danger or hurting anyone else. I could not get this message through to her. She insisted Mom had to listen, even when I told her that was impossible because she did not know she was not listening. Amy did not let it go.

When Mom first moved in with Amy and her family, I called every day to check up on them. The story was the same each day. Mom was still cutting up her clothing, still repeatedly washing and then hanging her clothes on the plants and small bushes outside the house because there was no line to hang the clothes on. A couple of hours later, she would pick the clothes up, fold them, and either put them in a drawer or suitcase or hide them somewhere in the house. She was still forgetting she had eaten and began stealing again. To cut down on the stealing, Amy stored most of the food in the cabinets. Mom began going into the cabinets and taking whatever she could get her hands on. Amy kept the fruit bowl on the countertop, and Mom ate whatever was in the bowl. It did not matter if there were three or ten fruits; she would eat them all. Amy loved plantains; Mom thought they were big bananas and ate them raw. Once she was finished eating the plantains, she hid most of the peels under the chairs and bed.

I knew Amy couldn't keep an eye on Mom 24/7. I advised her to put out a few fruits at a time and monitor them as best she could. That did not help much because Mom became adept at raiding the fridge and the cabinets. Finally, I told Amy to put a lock on the cabinets and fridge. What else could I suggest?

At night Mom got up several times to visit the bathroom. After being at Amy's for a couple of months, sometimes at night she forgot where the bathroom was. When she could not find the bathroom, she started urinating on the floor at the foot of her bed. This drove Amy crazy! Eventually she had to pick up the rug off the floor, but that did not stop the urinating; it continued on the wood floor.

To make the urinating situation worse, Mom drank water constantly. She would drink half a glass of water and go to her room. A few minutes later she would return, forget, and drink water again. Her brain was no longer telling her when she was not thirsty, so she drank all the time. If anyone told her she'd just had water, she refused to believe them. Amy continued trying to reason with her in vain.

Mom had now become an eating and drinking machine. She repeated the same behavior all day long. If it was not bolted or locked away, it became fair game for her.

SO MUCH ENERGY

Mom's bedroom in California was located on the first floor. She woke up quite early each morning, took several baths, dressed herself in many layers, put on her high heels, and headed out to the garden.

Amy and her family lived on a couple of acres in the mountains, so there were only a few houses in the general area. Mom was in her usual gardening mode. She would sweep as much of the garden as possible, then root up what little grass there was in the garden, pot and repot the plants, and dig as many holes as possible to plant what she deemed necessary.

She would water the plants constantly throughout the day. The plants must have breathed a sigh of relief when she went inside to find something to eat or inquire about the location of the bathroom. After completing these tasks, whatever was in her brain would rewind and she would start the entire process all over again, forgetting she had done the same thing less than ten minutes before.

There were no streetlights in the neighborhood. Once dusk approached Mom would go indoors because she had become afraid of the dark. Once she was inside her nightly routine would begin: eat, drink, and take several baths. After she dressed herself, she walked from window to window, looking curiously outside. We never found out exactly what she was looking for. This kept up until bedtime. Her energy level was off the scale; no matter how much work she did during the day, she just kept going. She never seemed to get tired.

She would go to bed around 10:00, and each night she would hang hand towels, clothing, and whatever else she found on the windows before getting into bed.

THE VISIT

Amy's best friend lives approximately two hours away from her. Amy visited her friend on a weekly basis, and Mom went along for the ride. When Mom was well and lived in California, she had also been friends with this lady. After Mom returned to California, she did not recognize the house when they went to visit. She insisted she had never been there before. The memory of the house, like so many other things, just vanished.

After church on Saturday, Amy's friend always hosted lunch for several people at the house. On one occasion, everyone sat down to eat, but as lunch progressed Amy noticed Mom was missing. Amy went looking from room to room but could not find Mom. She finally found her sitting on the porch in a bad mood. When pressed, Mom said she was looking for the bathroom and got lost. She could not remember how to get back into the house, so she decided to sit on the porch.

Amy had to take her back into the house to show her where the bathroom was. Amy rejoined the lunch crowd and assumed Mom would come back any minute. She began talking and forgot about Mom. Half an hour later Mom had not returned. Amy went searching again but did not find her in the bathroom; she looked unsuccessfully in several other places. She finally gave up and mentioned to her host that Mom was missing. Everyone joined in the hunt for Mom.

They finally located her in the host's bedroom. By this time the room had been rearranged: The bed was moved and the chest of drawers had no drawers because Mom had removed them and dispersed them around the room. The closet door was ajar and clothes were strewn all over the room; shoes were pulled off the rack and left all over the place. To say the least, the room was a mess.

Amy was extremely embarrassed. Mom had no idea how she had gotten into the room, much less that she had rearranged the décor.

FALLING FROM GRACE

For more than twelve years, Amy had a friend, Grace, who rented a room in her house. Grace was a nurse who always worked the night shift. She was single and did not want to be alone, so living with Amy and her family was a plus for her. Mom had lived in the house with Grace for many years, and they knew each other quite well. When Mom was well, she and Grace had always been in charge of cooking the meals for the family.

When Mom moved back to California, a few people at the church volunteered to assist in Mom's care to give Amy a needed break. They came by on Sunday and took Mom to the mall or on long rides.

By this time, Grace no longer lived with Amy. She had built her own home about ninety minutes away. When she found out about Mom's illness, she offered to take Mom for a week. She drove the ninety minutes and picked Mom up. Four days later, she called Amy to let her know she was bringing Mom back. She said something had happened and she was no longer willing to assist with Mom.

When Grace arrived she dropped Mom's bag in the living room and promptly left without saying anything. She never disclosed what had happened and thereafter stopped all communication with Amy. Amy tried contacting her several times, but never got a response. To this day we have no idea what Mom did. So, we moved on with yet another unanswered question and a longtime friendship in ruins for reasons no one understood.

MORE HELP

It had been six months since Mom moved to California. Each time I spoke with Amy, the conversation was the same.

Mom's memory was getting worse. She could no longer dial the phone. If the phone rang and no one was close to the phone, Mom was unable to recall how to pick up the receiver. If Amy got a phone call and walked out of the room, that old monster of thinking there were plots against her came back to life. She began accusing Amy of talking about her and trying to get rid of her. Mom was suspicious of everyone in the house. There were times when she refused to speak to Amy for days. If Amy was in one room, Mom would be in another room. Mom walked around the house on her tippy-toes as if she did not want anyone to know where she was. When anyone tried to reason with her, she began to scream at them.

I could not have a single conversation with Amy without her crying. At times the crying was downright pitiful. It did not matter what I said; I could not calm her down. It was clear to everyone that caring for Mom had overwhelmed her. Mom was still wearing as many things as she could comfortably put on. When Amy had to take Mom anywhere, instead of fighting with her about her clothes, she took her exactly the way she was. No matter how many dresses she had on, nothing was taken off. I am sure strangers wondered what was going on with them. But I understood how stubborn Mom could be, and poor Amy was on the verge of a nervous breakdown.

In addition to everything that was going on, Amy couldn't understand why God would allow Mom to lose her mind. She could not reconcile that a person who had such a difficult life would end up having such an awful end to her life. In fact, she just could not understand any of it and refused to listen to reason. Amy began fretting that Mom would not go to heaven because she had become such an awful person. I kept reminding her that anyone who truly believes in God knows that God in His wisdom does not deal with us the way we deal with one another. I could not convince her Mom would be afforded a place in heaven, and this made the situation even worse. Just imagine if you were religious all your life and all of a sudden you came to the realization that heaven for you was now lost. What would you do? This was Amy's predicament, so she continued to fuss, cry, and worry about the great unknown and the prospect of Mom going to hell. Sometimes I wanted to scream, "Who cares? We all are in hell right now, so what difference does it make if she eventually ends up there? She would just join the club!" But I refrained because I did not want to add to her sorrow.

Mom began asking to go home at the end of each day. Her focus was to go to her childhood home because somehow her brain was telling her that her parents were still alive. Each day she told us, "I want to go home." In addition to all the cleaning and washing, she also began washing her hands repeatedly, more than one hundred times a day. At the end of each day, she packed a little bag and was ready to leave. She would stand at the door with the bag in hand and tell anyone who was listening she was leaving. Once darkness came, she came back into the house and continued her vigil at the windows.

The following day it was the same thing all over again; she was a bundle of energy and never slowed down. Amy was about to lose it with her. She just could not take the same routine day in and day out. I was not sure what to do. When I brought up the subject of finding an affordable place in California to put Mom, Amy said no. I knew based on our conversations that she was at the end of her rope, but she was unwilling to do anything I suggested.

One day I found out by chance that a friend of the family who was living in California was out of work and asked if she would be willing to assist Amy with Mom. She agreed to do it short-term, as she had already planned to visit her family in another country for a few months.

We made the necessary arrangements and she moved in temporarily with Amy and her family. I was quite pleased with the situation and kept my fingers tightly crossed that Mom would be compliant and adjust to the new addition to the family.

Our friend soon learned Mom's routine of rising early, washing clothes, cleaning the house and yard, working in the garden, picking up the mail at the end of the long driveway, watering the garden, repotting the plants, watering the garden, and repotting the plants again and again. She was a constant companion to Mom, never allowing her out of her sight. Amy was getting a much-needed break from Mom, and that was a great relief to me.

Mom's trust issues were back, and she told Amy she did not trust her. When I spoke to Mom, she repeated the same thing to me. She no longer wanted to stay with Amy; she wanted to go to her brother. She began thinking her brother lived close by and could come and get her. I was instructed to make the necessary arrangements for her to leave. She had totally forgotten her brother lived in another country.

The relationship between Mom and Amy began to crumble. Several times they had heated arguments. Mom would get angry and start crying, proclaiming no one cared about her and that she was not a dog. She would storm out of the house and cry until she forgot what she was crying about. Mom was constantly angry, and if anyone asked why, she did not know. She now exploded over everything.

She began to refer to Amy as her sister. This added more frustration to the situation because as soon as she called Amy her sister, Amy would insist she was Mom's daughter. Mom would say Amy was too old to be her daughter, and an argument would begin over this.

Her negative comments toward Amy intensified. She started saying she had "a hard, dry-ass foot." She also began calling her a "fat bitch" and other choice insults.

Our friend had dealt with Alzheimer's clients before, so she was used to some of the behavior. However, Mom did things that she had not witnessed before.

Mom had met our friend a few years earlier. However, when she arrived, Mom did not remember her and began calling her "Ms. Muffin." Ms. Muffin, as she was called, assisted Amy for six weeks. Due to the location of the property, Ms. Muffin was concerned with the forestlike surroundings. If Mom was not being monitored and just wandered off into the woods, she would get lost and would be unable to find her way home. This was not a far-fetched idea; we know another family whose mother has this disease. One day she left the house, walked into the forest, got lost, and was never found.

One day Mom got up, did her morning routine, packed her little bag, and announced she was going home. Ms. Muffin and my brother-in-law were both in the yard; he was fixing something in his car and Ms. Muffin was keeping an eye on things. Mom came out of the house with the little bag and announced she was leaving. Ms. Muffin requested a kiss before she left; Mom complied, then told her she would not be seeing her again because she was never coming back to the house. Mom walked down the long driveway, passed the mailbox, crossed the street, and headed out to who knows where, all the time being shadowed by Ms. Muffin. After she crossed the street, Ms. Muffin ran after her and caught up with her.

Ms. Muffin then told Mom my uncle had just phoned saying he would come by and pick her up. It took a little convincing for her to talk Mom into coming back to the house. As soon as she arrived back at the house, the little bag was taken away and hidden. A few minutes later, Mom was in the garden as if nothing had occurred.

THE DEPARTURE

For six weeks Ms. Muffin took care of Mom. Amy seemed less stressed, and that made me very happy. When Ms. Muffin left, I became concerned about Amy, because she had once again begun her constant fussing with Mom. At the time, we were told that Ms. Muffin would return in a couple of months.

Once Mom and Amy were alone, the fighting and crying resumed. This time both of them would cry when I spoke to them. At least Amy knew why she was crying; Mom did not. She just kept repeating her old mantra of hating Amy.

Amy does not like to cook, and I had asked that Mom not be allowed to cook, so trips to the restaurant became particularly difficult; as soon as Mom finished her meal, she attempted to start cleaning the table. She also insisted she had to wash the dishes. When Amy explained they were not at home, Mom simply got angrier than usual. In fact, Mom now began to argue more and more with everyone no matter where they went. Back at the house she got lost more frequently.

When Amy visited her friends, that was another story: Mom would wait until people were not paying attention to her and slip away to begin rearranging whatever she found.

Because of the deteriorating relationship between the two, Mom began spending the entire day outside the house, puttering around in the garden.

When Mom received her meals, she began feeding portions to the animals. She would try to feed the dogs and cats vegetables, bread, or whatever was on her dinner plate. She was told the household pets did not eat table food, but quickly forgot and persisted with the practice. She always asked for milk for the cats, and if the milk was not given she would wait until Amy was in another room and steal the milk. Then she would pour it into any dish she could find and give it to the cat. It baffled her that the cat did not drink the milk. One day she took an entire stick of butter and gave it to the cat.

Although she stayed outside all day, at day's end she retreated into the house. Then she would begin rearranging her room. Each night she moved her bed several times. The drawers from the chest of drawers were pulled out and placed on the floor. She took all the clothes out of her closet and hung them all over the room. Once morning came, she would return all the items to their proper places.

When she ventured out of her room, she would move cautiously and deliberately, looking all around to avoid running into Amy. She would peek through doors and the corridors of the house. If she saw Amy in any room, she would quickly retreat to her bedroom, only to emerge a few minutes later, using the same secret-agent stealth techniques.

Mom now seemed to be retreating into her own world, and as she became more preoccupied in that world, the real one became less of a reality to her. The stress of Mom's illness, her behavior, and Amy's fussing were taking a huge toll on Amy's health.

I kept in touch with Ms. Muffin and secretly hoped she would return in a couple of months, but it took six months for that to happen. By the time she returned, Amy had completely fallen apart.

THE STROKE

Five months after Ms. Muffin's departure and ten months into Mom's living with Amy, they decided to visit a friend who lived in the mountains of Northern California. It was a six-hour drive.

Upon arriving, Mom found lots of things to occupy her time. Amy sat down and was having a conversation with her friend when suddenly she began slurring her words. Amy's husband is a research scientist and highly versed in the medical field. He instantly recognized the signs of a stroke and called 911. Amy was rushed to the hospital, where it was discovered she had three ruptured aneurysms in her brain.

She was hospitalized for a week. The doctors at the hospital told her she was very fortunate her husband had recognized the signs of a stroke and called 911 when he did. She got to the hospital within an hour of having the stroke. Had they waited, the effects of the stroke would have been much worse. The doctor referred to the time as "the golden hour." If one has a stroke and gets to the hospital within an hour, their prognosis is much better than most other stroke victims who do not seek treatment or who wait longer than an hour.

As a result of the stroke, Amy has problems with her memory and has been in therapy since. According to her doctor, she still has bleeding on her brain and has to be monitored closely going forward.

Mom stayed with Amy's friend while she was in the hospital. This was not an easy week for Amy's friend. It is one thing to have Mom for a day or two, but it is quite another to have her 24/7. Her constant energy and repetitive behaviors are enough to drive a sane person crazy. It is difficult to get her to listen. No matter what you say, she will tell you, "No, no, no, this is how I have been doing it for a long, long time." After Amy was released from the hospital, they stayed on at her friend's house for an additional week. Mom had no clue Amy was in the hospital. She never once asked where she was.

It was now apparent that if Ms. Muffin did not return to California soon, I would have to make alternate arrangements for Mom. I called Ms. Muffin to find out her plans. She was planning to return but, unfortunately for me, she did not have an exact date.

Stephen had previously contacted a couple of nursing homes in California on Mom's behalf. Prior to Amy's stroke, we had asked her to visit the nursing homes we had contacted in her area and make an assessment of the living conditions. She had always refused because she believed she would be able to care for Mom. After the stroke, we again bought up the subject. Amy said she would handle the situation. However, her stroke confirmed what I already knew: She could not handle Mom. Amy is a worrier by nature. She takes everything to heart and allows things to get to her quite easily. Now she had to get physical therapy and needed to see her doctors several times a week. She had to concentrate on getting better, and Mom, once again, had to be left out in the cold.

Stephen and I decided that in Amy's fragile state, Mom had to return to New Jersey.

Thankfully, Ms. Muffin returned a few weeks after Amy's stroke and resumed her daily care of Mom. A few weeks after Ms. Muffin's return, she and Mom were outside. Mom was in her gardening mode and Ms. Muffin was sitting on a bench in the garden. She must have heard or seen something because she looked over not far from where Mom was digging and saw a rattlesnake coiled up. Ms. Muffin quickly got Mom out of the garden, went back into the house, and told my brother-in-law. He went outside and killed the snake. A second snake appeared in the garden later that day. My brother-in-law did not kill this one; he joked that it was the mate of the one he had killed earlier in the day.

When I heard this story, I decided to accelerate Mom's return and made arrangements for her to come back in three weeks. I kept replaying the snake incident in my head and wondered what would have happened to Mom if Ms. Muffin had not been outside with her. I kept having visions of Mom being bitten, then falling down in the garden and dying because in her current state she didn't know the difference between a bird and a snake.

RETURN TO NEW JERSEY

I called and asked Ms. Muffin if she would be willing to relocate from California to New Jersey with Mom. After taking a few days to think it over, she agreed to move. I was overjoyed at the news. It was one less thing for me to do, and finding someone to care for Mom has always been almost impossible. The person has to have the patience of the Bible character Job. No matter what is thrown at them, they have to be able to carry on without getting upset.

Two months after Amy's stroke, Ms. Muffin and Mom were scheduled to come to New Jersey. After scouring several locations, Stephen and I rented the second floor of a two-family home within walking distance from Sally's home. If there was an emergency, I was twenty-five minutes away. I decided taking care of Mom would become a family project. Ms. Muffin had only been to New Jersey once before, and I needed her to feel as comfortable as possible. The apartment was fully furnished, which was a blessing to me because it was costing a pretty penny for the two of them to come to New Jersey.

We began cleaning and sprucing up the place. A week before Mom's arrival we began painting the apartment. To our horror, bugs started crawling out of the carpet, the furniture, the wall, and even the centerpiece. There were tiny bugs everywhere!

I had never seen bugs like this before. Sally's husband was helping us paint. He is a building engineer in New York City and therefore is quite familiar with all kind of bugs. He told us what he believed the bugs were, but then added if we killed one and it smelled bad, then they were bedbugs. We killed several bugs and the little things stank.

I lost my temper and called the landlady who lived on the first floor. I told her what we had found and strongly suggested she come upstairs immediately. When she arrived, I showed her the bugs. She kept saying bedbugs do not come out during the day and, furthermore, she had treated the place, and the bed had a protective cover on it. At this point, I began screaming at her, "You knew the apartment had bedbugs and never informed us!" She insisted the place had been treated and there were no bugs now. I kept screaming, reminding her that Mom is sick and she could get sicker if she came into a place that was infested with bedbugs. I was so angry I did not know what to do except scream.

We kept killing and picking up the bedbugs, because the landlady kept insisting there was no problem. I told everyone to drop whatever they were doing, and instructed them not to touch anything and to leave. Everyone, with the exception of Sally and Cindy, left. I told the landlady we were not going to move in and I wanted my rent and deposit back. Of course, she refused. She claimed we had changed things in the apartment without her knowledge. That got me even angrier. I just kept screaming she had rented the apartment to us under false pretenses. I handed her the keys and we left. In the end, she agreed to give back the first month's rent, but we lost the deposit and broker's fee. Instead of saving money, we ended up spending much more than we had anticipated.

I was now frantic. Mom and Ms. Muffin were coming in one week. We had to find an apartment and furnish it before their arrival. We began looking for a place but could not find anything in time. Therefore, it was decided they would stay with Stephen and me until a place was found. I knew Mom could not stay with Sally because her hatred for her had not changed, and I was still so afraid for Sally's safety.

The arrival day came, and as soon as I saw Mom I was shocked to see the way she looked. She had lost a lot of weight. Her neckbone was showing and her cheeks were sunken in; she looked really sick. If she was truly a thief and always stealing food, I could not understand where it was going. I could not get over how much she had changed in the time she had lived with Amy. I was never told of her weight loss and wondered what else could be going on with her. I thought maybe her cancer had returned. Who knew? In any event, something was not right with her; she really looked like she was starving.

She and Ms. Muffin moved in with us temporarily. I live in a suburban setting, and there is a streetlight close to the house. Mom did not seem as afraid of the darkness as she had been when she was in California. Her behavior changes also surprised me. Each day as the sun began to set, Mom seemed to change; her mood got a little darker. She began going from window to window, peering outside. She just kept moving from place to place, from the first floor to the second floor, opening up the blinds and looking out. When I asked her what she was looking for, she could not say. This would go on until we got her into bed many hours later. It was the strangest thing to watch—no matter what we said or did, we could not get her to stop. It seemed she was driven by some unseen being that had total control over her.

During the day, she would constantly open the tap and wash her hands. She washed her hands at least twenty times an hour. When she was not washing her hands, she wanted to cook. When she got up in the morning, she wanted to cook—during the day she wanted to cook, and in the afternoon the desire to cook was overwhelming. She would walk over to me and say, "You know, the boys are coming home soon and will need something to eat. I am going to the kitchen to cook." I would tell her we had already cooked, but to the kitchen she would go. She would open the cabinets, take out the pots and fill them with water, put them on the stove, and then ask me for the matches to light the stove.

I was glad she had forgotten how to turn the stove on herself. One day she walked over to the stove and turned the knob on. The burner did not light and the gas just flowed, and within a couple of minutes the entire house smelled of gas. This scared me half to death because as far as she was concerned she was cooking, yet here she was endangering herself and everyone else in the house.

The first Sunday she and Ms. Muffin were at the house, I wanted to keep her busy. I was trying to see if I could get her out of her routine, so I asked her to help me prepare chicken for dinner.

I am very picky when it comes to meat; it has to be cleaned and washed before it is cooked. I had to give her instructions on how to wash and clean the fat off the chicken. A few minutes later, I was distracted and walked away. Upon returning to the kitchen, I noticed she had cut her finger and did not realize it was bleeding. When I asked what had happened, she could not tell me. I thanked her for the help and told her I would finish up. I then washed her hand, gave her a bandage, and told her to keep pressure on her finger to stop the bleeding.

She did not complain about the cut at all. I asked her if it was hurting and she said no. Once I had her seated, she had forgotten about the chicken incident. It was just so sad; it broke my heart. There was a time when Mom cooked for a family of fourteen. Now she couldn't even wash a small piece of chicken without cutting herself. It was the last time I asked her to assist me in the kitchen.

THE NEW APARTMENT

Stephen and I finally found another apartment for Mom and Ms. Muffin. It was approximately eight minutes away from Sally and thirty minutes from me. This allowed Cindy and Sally to visit Mom on a regular basis. This proximity was important because, at the time, Ms. Muffin could not drive.

It was now the last week in August 2013. There had been so much drama in the past few weeks, I was secretly wishing I would get a break and everything would work out well in this new place.

My wish was not granted.

The apartment had to be furnished. We placed the furniture order and the delivery came in a few days. Once the furniture was in the apartment, we moved their clothes in and unpacked. The apartment complex was situated well off the main road, nestled in a lovely tree-lined community. It was a fairly well-contained facility covering many blocks, and it was well lit at night. Lights came on automatically as twilight slipped in; the front of each residence was bathed in lights. This also gave me the assurance that nothing bad would happen to them. There was a security car that drove through the entire complex several times throughout the night.

The first night at the apartment passed fairly uneventfully. Mom was her usual self, getting restless as darkness slipped in. Of course, she did her routine of pacing back and forth, looking through the windows, wanting to cook, and going through the closets.

On the second night something drastically changed. As darkness approached, Mom went upstairs, packed a small bag, came downstairs, and announced she was going home to see her parents. Wanting to see her parents was not something new, but this time she approached the door and tried to open it. Ms. Muffin had to stand in her way. This made Mom extremely angry, and she began cursing. Prior to this she would curse once in a while, but this was different. She started using the f-word and told Ms. Muffin to get the fuck out of her way. I was told it was a very ugly scene. When Mom realized she would not be allowed to open the door, she went back upstairs. In a few minutes she descended the stairs again, trying to leave. This went on for more than half the night. She finally went to bed at 2:00. At 6:00 she was up; she got out of bed, took her shower, and went back to her old self. The desire to escape had vanished.

However, on this particular morning her routine intensified. The handwashing was now every minute or so, and every other word she spoke was an expletive. She took an entire roll of toilet paper apart and folded each piece in tiny squares. She began saying she would hit people—or worse, shoot them. Not only did she wish to shoot them, but she specified she was going to shoot them just under the waistline. She formed her hand and fingers into the shape of a gun and said, "Pow." She said she was going to get a knife and use it on someone. She told Ms. Muffin she had to leave, and if she did not allow her to leave, she was going to break the window and jump out. It was scary.

The third night she became a raving lunatic. She packed her clothes once again and was ready to leave. She came down the steps to leave, and when Ms. Muffin would not let her out of the apartment, all hell broke loose. Mom began screaming and tried to push Ms. Muffin out of the way to get access to the door. When Ms. Muffin refused to budge, Mom began threatening her. She could not stay still. She kept moving like a caged animal; she wanted to leave and it seemed nothing or no one was going to stop her. She kept walking all through the apartment cursing.

It got so scary Ms. Muffin called Sally for help. Sally, Cindy, my nephew Brett and Tara came over. None of them could calm Mom down. She was frantically trying to get out the front door, all the while holding on to the little yellow plastic bag in her hand. She kept cursing and saying she had to go home. She went to the kitchen at one point and found a knife, and when she returned to the living room she threatened to use it on Brett. It took a combined effort to get the knife away from her.

At midnight, when they could not get her into bed, they called my house, but I did not hear the phone. They called from midnight to 2:00 a total of five times. The portable air conditioner was on in my room and I never heard the phone ringing. Cindy taped the episode on her phone. When she showed it to me, I was horrified. It was like a scene from the movie *The Exorcist*. The only thing Mom did not do was vomit on everyone, but bodies were being pushed around, her voice sounded very deep, and her eyes looked as though they were encircled with something black. She just looked awful.

Four adults tried to get her in bed and could not. In desperation, they told her she was going to be given a candy and gave her a dose of an over-the-counter sleep medication instead. Nothing happened. Half an hour later they administered another dose—still nothing. She was given a total of three doses and still nothing happened; it did not get her sleepy. Everyone felt so powerless because nothing seemed to slow her down.

She was still ranting when Brett left at 2:00. She kept the rest of the ladies up until 4:00. She finally went to bed, but two hours later she was up, fully recharged and raring to go. Once she was up and out of bed, she reverted to her old forgetful self.

The following day, I bought some herbal sleep aid and brought it to the apartment. Before it got dark, I took her for a long walk, assuming it would tire her out and she would sleep better. We walked for approximately two hours and returned to the apartment. She went directly upstairs, packed her bags, came down, and told me, "Let's go!"

"Where are we going?" I asked.

"Home."

I told her she was home and she yelled, "I was just at home! You brought me to this place, and if you do not take me back, I will just walk back by myself!"

She again headed for the door, and we had to stand in her way. As before, she began cursing and calling us names: "I will fuck the both of you up if you do not get out of my way." When she could not get out the door, she threatened again to break the window and jump out.

At night she became so hostile that most of my family members were afraid of her. She started pacing around in circles with the little plastic bag in her hand. We could not get her to sleep. These episodes continued for several days; we dreaded the nights.

A few days later, Ms. Muffin told me she would not be able to take care of Mom in the state she was in. We needed to put her on medication. I never wanted to put Mom on medication and tried all types of herbal alternatives to avoid it. Nothing worked.

When we first realized something was wrong with Mom, I began taking classes to become a nutritionist, specializing in herbs. It took me two years to complete the classes and another year to study for the eleven tests in order to become certified. When I was almost finished with the classes, I asked my teacher what I could give Mom to help with her memory problem. She looked me in the eye and said, "Nothing." I refused to believe her.

A friend of mine, who is a nurse, suggested I take Mom to the hospital and tell them what was going on. Mom needed to be evaluated, and once this was done they could prescribe some type of medication to calm her down. It seemed Mom's illness had now morphed into the bizarre. Initially, when she began behaving badly after their arrival in New Jersey, I assumed her disease had gone into another phase and in a week or two she would be back to her old self. After all, Ms. Muffin had told me when they were in California, Mom would always say she was going home and try to leave, but she always slept at night. Unfortunately, this was no longer the case.

Stephen's maternal grandmother suffered from Alzheimer's. Before Mom left California, Stephen and I had been warned by my mother-in-law that changing Mom's surroundings would cause her to become extremely anxious. Unfortunately, the move from California to our house and then to the apartment was too much for her, and it caused far more trouble than we had anticipated.

I was reluctant to put Mom on medication because I had seen what it could do to other people. It was not my desire to medicate her with drugs that prevented her from functioning. I kept reassuring Ms. Muffin that this phase would pass, but unfortunately for all of us, it did not.

DECISIONS 2013

As the months passed and Mom became steadily worse, my husband and I decided it was time to find outside day care for her. We needed her to get out of the house, and we thought some outside activities would do her (and us) a world of good. Caring for her was becoming monumental for everyone involved, especially Ms. Muffin.

We secured outside day care for her. Initially it was two days a week; within three weeks it was increased to five days. The day care center was twenty-five minutes away from where they lived. By this time, Ms. Muffin had gotten her driver's license, and she and Cindy took turns driving her. Upon arrival, Mom would announce, "I am not going in there." She had to be convinced to go in to the day care center. Cindy and Ms. Muffin would wait about a minute after her pronouncement about not going in, then they would try again. On some mornings it was an easy task, but other times it took a lot of effort to get her out of the car.

She had become strong-willed, and never seemed to forget about not wanting to do something. How funny that she could remember to be strong-willed. Once in the building, she would say to Cindy or Ms. Muffin, "You are *not* leaving me here." They assured her she was not going to be left behind. Once they got to the reception area, the day care workers would greet Mom quite warmly: "B, how about a hug and a kiss?" Once the hugging and kissing began, Cindy or Ms. Muffin would turn and leave.

One day Cindy went to pick Mom up, but when they tried to leave the center, the front door alarm tripped. Several of the workers came over and patted Mom down, attempting to locate the detection tag that each participant in the program wore. The workers did a general pat-down and came up empty-handed. They told Mom to go through the door again; when she did, the alarm tripped again.

"I bet you it's down there," Cindy said, pointing to the lower portion of Mom's body. The workers were very skeptical. Cindy insisted that Mom had hidden the tag in her underclothes. The workers politely asked Mom to walk back to the office with them. Mom, eager to please them, agreed. She placed her hands on her waist and strutted off as if walking on a runway as she disappeared into another room with the workers.

After several minutes of strip-searching, the workers found the metal tag safely tucked away in Mom's underwear, to their disbelief! When they got back to the reception area and told Cindy where they had found the tag, her response was, "I told you it was there." Everyone just shook their heads.

THE DENTIST

So many things are not working well for Mom. A couple of months ago, she was having a problem with a tooth. She never told us it was bothering her; she got up one morning and her face was swollen. She must have been in pain because the tooth was infected. We went to her dentist, but unfortunately she had to be recommended to someone else. When I called the other office, I explained to the receptionist Mom had Alzheimer's and gave them a laundry list of all the things they had to do just to be able to see her. The young lady must have thought I was crazy. How can you call a dentist and say this person is coming to see you, but she may not open her mouth? If I were on the other end of the line, I would think the person calling was nuts. You are going to see the dentist, he or she specializes in teeth, teeth are in the mouth—and one must open his or her mouth to give the dentist access to the teeth. Because I believed she would not understand what to do once she arrived, I had to ask that she be sedated.

When Mom got to the dentist's office, she did not want to sit down; she wanted to go home. She was first told it was raining and she couldn't go outside. A minute later, it was the same request: "I want to go home." The same excuse was made, with an added detail: that the rain had turned into a full-blown storm with thunder and lightning. One excuse after another was made just to keep her calm. She actually believed she was hearing the thunder.

Once she saw the dentist, she commented how cute he was. He spoke to her and calmed her down. He did not think it was necessary to put her to sleep; the only problem was that she kept forgetting to keep her mouth open. The appointment dragged on for over two hours. Finally, she was finished and they headed home. For the rest of the day she did not mention the dentist again, nor did she say she had any pain from the long procedure.

The following day we went to church. On the way back, Mom was making her usual comments, when suddenly she said, "You know, I went to the dentist yesterday."

I was surprised she still remembered. "What did he do?" I asked.

She said she could not remember. But it made me smile that every once in a while some little hiccup sparked life into her memory. Remembering the dentist visit more than fifteen hours after it occurred was indeed an accomplishment worth celebrating.

My joy was short-lived because she never mentioned going to the dentist again; the entire episode vanished for her. Just as quickly as the memory came, it was gone.

WEEKLY VISITS

Each week, I try to go over to see Mom one night after work. I leave work an hour early, ride the train for fifty minutes to one hour, then drive the thirty minutes to the apartment. One night when I arrived she was having dinner. I greeted Ms. Muffin, Cindy, and Tara. Mom did not seem to recognize me and simply kept eating. I reached over and touched her on her shoulder. She turned and looked my way but said nothing. I walked into the kitchen and got some water for myself. Upon returning, I said, "Hello, B." She said hi and smiled.

I sat down and asked how her day was. "I did not do much except walk around," she answered. She began relaying an incident to me, but less than a minute into her story she changed the subject and started talking about something that made absolutely no sense.

There was an empty bottle on the table, and she picked it up and asked me if there was water in it. I told her the bottle was empty and she gave me a funny look. She refused to believe it was empty. She then removed the cover from the bottle and tried to drink from it; when nothing came out, she looked at me again.

We continued sitting at the table. Tara was sitting on the living room sofa softly singing to herself. Mom wanted to know who the second person was who was sitting on the sofa next to Tara. Puzzled, I told her Tara was sitting by herself. Mom said in disbelief, "No. I see someone sitting with her, but I cannot see the person's face. Don't you see the person with their back to us just sitting there?"

There was no one else sitting on the sofa.

DECISIONS, DECISIONS

To assist Ms. Muffin, I began visiting the apartment more often. On this particular day, I arrived around 6:00. The staircase to the second floor was just a couple feet away from the front door. When I entered the apartment, I saw Mom sitting on the steps in her PJs with a small plastic bag next to her.

"Hello, B," I greeted her.

She snapped at me, "Where the hell have you been? I have been waiting here for you for a long time." She got up and picked up her little bag. "Let's go."

"Go where?"

"Let's go home."

"We are home. I came to see you," I reminded her.

She began to scream, "You horrible bitch! I am going home to see my Mom and Dad. I am leaving!"

When I told her a second time she *was* home, she turned and started coming toward me. I raised my voice and called her name several times, telling her to stop. I was sure she was going to hit me, but I made up my mind not to back down. I wanted her to see I was not afraid of her. For the first time in my life, I decided if Mom took a swing at me, I would hit her and hit her very hard. I decided the best way to knock her down was to hit her in her midsection; she kept coming and I kept yelling her name. Eventually, I took a couple of steps back and she finally just stood her ground and stopped coming toward me.

When it was all over, I felt so guilty that I had been prepared to knock her to the ground. I was prepared to hit Mom because I could not reason with her, and this was all because of this terrible disease.

THE SLAP

Each day, Cindy picked Tara up from school and brought her to the apartment. She was keeping Ms. Muffin company and helping out with Mom as much as she could. By this time, I assumed Mom was starting to believe that Tara, who was now eleven, was me!

As night approached, Mom again started pacing and asking to go home; but on this particular night she packed two little bags and descended the stairs. When she got to the bottom of the stairs, she called out to Tara and instructed her, "Come take your bag and let's go home."

Tara was seated in the dining room doing her homework. She looked up and said to Mom, "Granny, my mom will come and pick me up later and take me home." Mom responded by cursing, telling her to get her fucking self up and come over to her so they could leave. Tara was halfway through her sentence when Mom walked over to her and slapped her extremely hard on her face. Tara began to cry.

Ms. Muffin and Cindy ran over to the table and stood between Mom and Tara because Mom seemed poised to slap her a second time. When I was told of the incident, I again tried to reassure the ladies that Mom would revert to her "old" self and the violent tendencies would cease. We continued giving her a natural sleep aid nightly, which was completely ineffective. I kept telling Ms. Muffin she had to give the natural stuff time to work because it was not drugs and it needed a longer period of time to take effect. Deep in my heart, I believed the natural stuff would work.

A couple of days later, it was raining very hard. As night approached, Mom once again summoned Tara to leave. Tara told Mom that Stephen and I would be coming over in a few minutes to get her. Mom adores my husband, and I guess Tara assumed if she used his name Mom would not get upset.

Mom walked over to the dining area. In the corner of the room there was a large umbrella stand with several umbrellas in it. Mom picked up the biggest umbrella by the handle and began walking toward Tara. As soon as Tara saw her coming, she got up from her chair and moved to the other side of the table away from Mom. When Mom saw this, she said she would "break her ass." Cindy and Ms. Muffin had to intervene once again. Mom became frustrated when she realized she could not get to Tara and banged the umbrella on the table. Everyone was startled by the sound of the umbrella hitting the table. To defuse the situation, Tara was taken home.

After this incident, I gave specific instructions that Tara should not be around her grandmother. I became fearful that Mom would hurt her. Thereafter, Tara became more afraid of Mom.

As usual, Mom was fine during the day, but that nocturnal beast came out as soon as darkness approached.

I think my entire family became wary of Mom, even though I explained to my niece that Grandma was ill and really did not hold any ill will toward her or anyone else. It was just the illness and this phase would soon go away. But it is awfully difficult for an eleven-year-old to reconcile that with the night creature that kept coming after her.

Mom became fearless at night. She did not seem to worry about anything. Her only concern was getting home to her mother and father, and it did not matter what was said—she was going home, but home where? She had lived in the United States for decades, and her parents' home was thousands of miles away in another country. Her parents were dead, but she did not remember this. In her head, her home was within walking distance of the apartment, and she was going to get there no matter what.

My friend again urged me to put Mom on medication, and I began to see the wisdom in her suggestion. I remained skeptical about mind-altering drugs being given to Mom, but she was rapidly becoming a threat to both herself and those around her. Tara had to be hidden when she came to the apartment. Mom had to be distracted while they sneaked her into the apartment and locked her in Ms. Muffin's room. Cindy was also afraid of her. And poor Ms. Muffin—well, my heart went out to her because she was the one who had to care for Mom night and day.

It was now mid-September, less than a month since Mom had returned from California, and no one could control her. Even though she did not understand the consequences of, nor could she remember, what she had done, her actions determined what we all did. Everyone actively tried to stay out of her way and tried not to upset her. Whatever she wanted, within reason, we gave her just to keep her calm.

Mom always loved long drives. She was now taken out of the house before nightfall for drives or long walks. We hoped that if it got dark when she was outside the house, then upon her return she would think she had gone home. In the car, she was preoccupied with the houses and car headlights flashing by; she looked out the window without saying anything.

I recall taking her for a two-hour walk one evening. On our way back to the apartment, my feet were killing me. I asked if she was tired, and she said, "Nope." I even asked if her feet were okay. "Yes," she replied. She just kept doing the Energizer Bunny routine, only needing a couple of hours' sleep. It was almost like she was manic. How could she get so little sleep yet go one hundred miles per minute each day without getting tired?

Something had to be done to address this problem long-term. Finally, on a Friday afternoon, with tears streaming down my face, I acted on my friend's advice. I finally decided that if I did not do something she might kill herself, or kill one of us. But my greatest fear now was for Tara.

THE HOSPITAL

I took a day off from work and spent the day with Mom at my house. I was still hoping not to put her on medication.

I decided to conduct an experiment. I asked Mom to help me clean up the gardens. I have two little gardens at the front of my house and a larger one at the rear of the house. It takes hours of work to tidy them up.

We tackled the rear garden first. She walked into the garden and just stood there, looking somewhat perplexed. I instructed her to pull up the weeds and all the plants that were dying. She asked me to show her how to pull up the weeds. I showed her how to pull the weeds from the bottom and then leave them on the ground to be picked up later when we were finished clearing.

We worked for about fifteen minutes, then I went inside to get a napkin because I was sweating. Upon my return, I noticed Mom was standing with some grass in her hands. "What is the matter?" I asked her.

"I don't know what to do with the grass."

I showed her where to put the grass. She walked over to the patio and placed the grass in a very neat pile that she had started prior to my going inside. She had the grass and plants separated by length and size. This was another habit she had adopted; everything had to be neatly organized.

If she was washing dishes, everything had to be arranged in linear fashion by size. When she folded clothes, she did so military style; no crinkles could be found on them. If she found any crinkle, she would begin refolding. She was now transferring the same mannerisms to the grass and plants.

She also did not remember how to put the grass in the bag, I had to show her how to do it. I put some in so she could see what to do.

After my demonstration, she casually walked over to the longest pile of plants, took a small portion, and broke it into two pieces while taking another piece of plant and slowly wrapping it around the little pile she had broken. When she was done wrapping the little piles, she took the remaining excess and neatly tucked it into the wrapped section. The little piles were so neat that they looked like large loaves of bread.

I was beginning to wonder if Mom was possessed by some unseen neat-freak spirit. She continued to wrap the piles and place them in the bag. When the bag was finally full, the piles reminded me of little gifts rather than grass and plants. It was just unbelievable that she had wrapped up everything so nice and tidy.

We worked outside that day for about four hours. I kept asking her if she was tired, and she always answered no. When we were finished, we went into the house and cleaned up.

We had something to eat and Mom began walking around. It was now around 4:00, and her demeanor started to change. The terrible version of her began to emerge; she started moving around so much I finally decided to take her to the emergency room. The hospital is less than a mile away from my house. I told her we were going to see the doctor. We got into the car and drove to the hospital.

I was a wreck. I cried all the way there. I could not understand what had happened to Mom. Why could we no longer reason with or reach her no matter what we did?

I parked the car and we walked into the emergency room. I explained to the receptionist why we were there. I said that Mom was sick and at night we could not control her; she became violent and uncontrollable. The receptionist typed a few things into her computer and asked Mom's name. Mom had stayed at this hospital previously, so as soon as her information was entered into the system her record came up. The receptionist asked about the insurance coverage and I handed over the card. As the card left my hand, it occurred to me we were about to start a new chapter in her life.

We sat down and waited to be called. At around 5:30 the nurse finally called us. She asked Mom a few questions, none of which she could answer. I explained her behavior to the nurse and said for the first time since Mom got ill that I needed to put her on medication. As you can imagine, this was difficult for me to admit. I finally realized I could not help her with any alternative options. This made me feel quite defeated. For years I had tried to help her, and here I was waving the white flag, finally admitting to myself and everyone else there was nothing I could do for her. I wanted to cry my eyes out. Defeat is a terrible thing.

We were sent to another part of the emergency room and led into a tiny room. There was a curtain that could be pulled around the bed for privacy. It was now after 7:00, and the nocturnal traveler had already reared her head. Mom kept saying she had to go, and kept heading for the big doors that led out to the waiting area. She refused to sit down and no one could calm her down. A few minutes after 7:00, Stephen arrived and began walking her up and down the hallway.

The hospital assigned a social worker, who came in about half an hour later. I began answering her questions and started to cry again. I explained everything to the social worker; letting her know about Mom's poor memory and that she had just returned to New Jersey. I also told her about the violent outbursts and her nightly insistence on going home. We were still deep in conversation in the hallway when Mom and Stephen passed by for perhaps the hundredth time.

As they walked by, I could hear Mom telling Stephen she had to go home and insisting he allow her to go out the door. Stephen held her hand to prevent her from going too far, but she now began pulling away from him. The emergency room doctor came over and asked what was wrong. I tried to explain, but my crying made that difficult. Stephen had to step in and speak to the doctor.

The doctor then said she has "sundowning." It was the first time I had heard this term. What the hell was this diagnosis? I would later learn that many sufferers of this disease have this syndrome.

The social worker recommended that Mom be placed in the psychiatric ward for evaluation and also for medication therapy until she calmed down. Mom was finally admitted and placed in another room in the emergency room, as there were no beds available in the psychiatric unit. They indicated it might take a day or two to get a bed for her. It was way past our bedtime and I suggested to Stephen that he go home. Once he left, I assumed I would be able to lock the door to the room to keep Mom inside. I guess the joke was on me because I found out quite quickly that in the emergency room, as long as a patient is in a room, the door cannot be locked. Who knew? Well, we had to go to plan B, which I must confess I had not yet formulated.

Now that she was admitted, she was required to change into a hospital gown and remove her street clothing. By the time we got the gown it was almost midnight and I was exhausted. I walked over to Mom with the gown in hand and told her she needed to put it on. I told her I would assist her. As we began taking off her clothing, I noticed she was wearing one dress, two bras, and three panties. We removed everything with the exception of one pair of panties. I then assisted her with the gown and tied the two little strings in the back.

We were alone in the room. Mom began talking to herself and started trying to undo the gown. "B, you are not allowed to take the gown off," I told her.

These words sent her into a rage. She began cursing, "You fucking bitch! Who the hell do you think you are telling me what to do? What makes you think I will listen to a little fucking bitch like you?" Even as she was spouting her Shakespearean lines, she was trying to undo the gown. It was a sight to behold: hands behind her head as she kept walking around the room cursing. Finally, the gown came off and there she stood in only her underwear.

I was shocked she would do something like this. I raised my voice slightly and told her to put the gown back on. I began walking toward her to assist her. She glared at me menacingly, raised her hand, and pointed at me. "Do not touch me, because if you do, I will fuck you up here tonight."

I stopped in my tracks but kept asking her to please put the gown on. I turned around and faced the door and told her there was a man across the hall from her room and he was watching her.

"Do you think I give a fuck about who is watching me? Let him fucking watch. I don't fucking care." She then took the gown and put it back on, but she decided the opening had to be in the front instead of in the back. I tried telling her the opening had to be in the back to give the doctors easy access when they came to examine her. She said to me, "When you were little, I did not like you, but now that you are grown, I truly hate you."

I broke down and cried. It was one thing when she told other people she hated them, but she had never said this to me before. I just stood there watching her trying to tie the gown as tightly around her as possible. This activity kept her busy for approximately fifteen minutes. She was a monster. Why had she become this awful?

She kept tying and untying the gown because the front ends did not match. When she saw she could not make the ends match, she muttered some curse words to herself and finally gave up. I assumed something clicked in her head because— for the first time, I think—she noticed the open door. I was standing at the door, and because she was still angry with me, I assumed she would not want to pass me. There was a second door on the other side of the room that was closed. She walked over to that door and attempted to open it, and when the knob on the door did not turn, she began to curse again, this time at the door.

Mom kept saying she had to go home. She headed in my direction, but I did not move. "You are in the hospital and you are not allowed to leave this room until the doctor comes to see you," I told her.

"Fuck you and the doctor. I am going to fucking rip your head off, you fucking bitch! Move or I will move you myself." So, being the good daughter that I've always claimed to be, I moved out of her way, and out the door she went—down the hallway, past the nurses' station.

I requested assistance from the nurse: "Mom is trying to escape." The nurse got up, came over and took Mom by the hand, and told her she had to go back to her room because there were too many sick people around.

Because Mom was not listening, the nurse prescribed a sleeping pill for her. It was given to her, and back into the room we went. She repeated, "I have to leave," and once again she warned me to get out of her way. I moved and out she went again. There was a security guard nearby. I asked for his assistance. When a stranger spoke to Mom, she listened.

The security guard asked me her name. When he called her name, she turned around with a big smile and faced him. "How do you know my name?" As she made her way toward him, I was stunned at the change in her attitude. Mom had been cursing at me less than a minute ago, and now she was so angelic to this total stranger.

The security guard asked Mom to go back to her room and she obliged. In less than two minutes, she had forgotten all about staying in the room. Still fumbling with the gown, she told me to get the fuck out of her way, and if I didn't, she would break my fucking leg just under my knee so that I would be unable to walk. Again I moved out of the way. She walked out the door with me in tow because I had to be sure she did not get out of the automatic door at the end of the hallway. When she was a few feet away from the automatic door, I ran past her and stood in front of the door. Still cursing, she turned around and headed in the opposite direction, saying, "You cannot keep me here, bitch."

This routine continued for almost two hours. The nurse helped me again. This time, after one hour had passed and the sleeping pill was showing no sign of working, the nurse gave her an injection and left us in the room. As soon as the nurse left, Mom got up and out of the room she went. I asked several people to help me get her back in the room.

At 2:00, with the sleeping pill and injection still not working, the nurse told me I should leave. She said that perhaps Mom would behave better with a total stranger around, and she would have someone sit in front of Mom's door because she was going to be admitted to the psychiatric ward, and this was the normal protocol for those patients. Before I left, the nurse told me they would give Mom a stronger sleep medication. She was positive the third medication would put her to sleep. It was beyond explanation how Mom had been given a sleeping pill and a shot, and nothing had happened.

I left the emergency room a little after 2:00, both physically and mentally drained. For as long as I live, I will not understand what had possessed Mom and why she had become so cruel and unkind.

THE VISIT

The following morning I returned to the hospital at 8:00. Mom was still in her room. An aide was sitting in front of the room with a chart, guarding the door. She said she had to monitor Mom's behavior and keep a log of what was going on with her.

When I glanced into the semi-lit room, Mom was lying on her back, asleep with her mouth open. She looked so helpless and pitiful that I started to cry.

As I was watching Mom in bed, a man was wheeled into the general area strapped to a bed. The smell of his bodily waste filled the room. He called out for someone named Jean. He later requested a hammer and ladder; I assumed in his younger days he must have been in the construction industry. He kept calling Jean. It was such a sorrowful sight that it made me cry even more. Here was a man who had probably worked hard and been independent all his life, and now he seemed destined to end his days as he had started them, in diapers. I tried unsuccessfully to tune him out, but his situation touched me so deeply because I realized that I knew what his loved ones were going through. He just kept calling Jean. A person was assigned to watch him, but where could he go? He was already strapped to the bed.

The new "watcher" became Jean. "Jean," he kept saying, "bring me the hammer. Jean bring this or that. Jean, Jean, Jean . . ." It went on for hours.

About an hour or so after I arrived, Mom woke up and asked to go to the bathroom. I told the aide I would take her. I walked toward her and noticed she was having trouble getting up. In fact, she was extremely groggy. I assisted her out of bed. She leaned against me and we began to walk out of the room. Gone was the need to go home, and gone was that awful person from the night before.

We reached the bathroom, and I helped Mom get on the toilet. I felt so sorry for her because she had no idea where she was. The nocturnal creature was gone now that it was daylight. We slowly walked back to her room and I helped her back into bed. Within five minutes, she had fallen into a deep sleep. I knew she was heavily medicated.

After waiting another hour, the social worker from the previous night arrived and informed me a bed had become available in the psychiatric ward. Several different medications would be tried to see which one would calm her down. Her stay in the hospital would be between five and seven days.

After the social worker left, I woke Mom up because she had not had anything to eat since the previous day. I tried feeding her some lunch, but she was not very interested in the food. I insisted she eat. She tried but was not successful. About an hour later, the attendant arrived with a wheelchair and she was taken away.

I was going to accompany her, but the nurse explained to me that visiting hours in the psychiatric ward were from 6:00 to 8:00 each day, no exceptions. The doors were locked from the inside, and packages or bags coming into the unit had to be thoroughly inspected. They had strict rules regarding the number of visitors in the room—only two at a time. I was told to come back during visiting hours, and they gave me the room number. I left and, once again, cried all the way home.

I went home and tried to rest, but rest did not come. I kept picturing Mom and wondering what was going to happen to her. I was so scared for her—and, I must confess, that feeling has never left me.

VISIT II

When I returned to the hospital that evening, I was not sure what to expect. This was the bewitching hour when the restlessness awoke in her and she wanted to run. I took one bag with me that included a change of clothing and toiletries.

To get to the psychiatric unit, one had to go to a designated floor and walk down a long hallway. A security guard stood just before the entrance door. I had to sign in and write down the patient's name I was visiting. The guard pointed to the door and instructed me to ring the bell, which I did. A voice came over the intercom, asking, "Who are you here to visit?" I said Mom's name and the buzzer rang; I pushed the heavy double door to gain access.

Once inside, I was told where I could locate Mom. I walked down another hallway and found her room. The nurses had boldly written her name in uppercase letters, BARBARA, on a large white piece of paper and hung it on the door. There were two beds in the room, but they were both empty. Mom was nowhere to be found. I walked back to the nurses' station and was told I would find Mom walking somewhere on the floor. I asked the nurse about the name on the door and was told Mom had forgotten her room while wandering the floor.

I walked down the opposite hallway and found Mom ambling around. She saw me and exclaimed, "What the hell took you so long?"

"I came soon as I could."

"Let's go home. These people in this big house are treating me very badly and refuse to let me leave." She took me by the hand. "Let's go."

"We are not allowed to leave," I told her.

Once I said that, she backed away a little. I did not want to get her upset, so I told her we had to take a shower. "I don't want a bath, I want to go home."

"Home where?" I inquired.

She quickly named the place of her birth. "I have to go to see my parents because they are waiting for me, and I don't want to be late."

I took her by the hand. "Let's go for a walk." I walked her back to her room.

There was a huge window next to her bed. She examined the windows carefully and said she was sure she could break the window and jump out. We were on the seventh floor. It did not seem to matter to her what floor it was; she assured me she could break the window and simply jump out. "I can jump pretty high." She pointed to the street that ran alongside the hospital. "That is Cortez Terrace," she said. That was where she had lived prior to moving to the United States. "If you walk down there and turned the corner, we would be home."

I changed the subject to her taking a bath.

"I've already taken a bath," she insisted. I took her to the bathroom just a few steps away from her room and helped her undress. She had a name tag on her wrist and kept pulling at the tag. "I got this some time ago and I need you to help me remove it."

I explained to her she was in the hospital and the wristband was her identification. She just looked at me; I knew she had no idea what I was talking about.

While taking her bath, she told me one of her friends had visited her the previous day. I knew it was just another misplaced fantasy. No one had visited. She was seeing things thousands of miles away, and worse, they were long gone and I couldn't convince her otherwise. I could not even convince her she was in the United States. When I told her we were in New Jersey, she said, "I used to visit there a very long time ago."

After the shower we returned to her room. I put a pair of pajamas and a robe on her. I wanted to be sure she would not be cold because she does not like to use any covers while sleeping.

I asked if she was cold, and she replied, "No." In the drawer I left one nightgown, one pair of panties, and one robe. I did not want to leave too much behind because I knew if I did, she would put everything on and I would have a difficult time taking it all off.

I tried talking to her, but she was focused on going home and that was the only subject she wanted to discuss. A bell rang and a voice came over the speaker system: Visiting hours would be over in five minutes. I said to her, "I have to leave. I promise I will be back tomorrow."

She told me the man across the hall made a lot of noise and she couldn't stay there. She insisted I take her with me.

"I will take you home as soon as the doctor give the go-ahead." I began to leave the room, and behind me I heard her say, "But you can't leave me here." I walked away and moved up the hall toward the locked double doors.

She came behind me again, insisting that the people there were not nice to her and she was never going to return to this big house.

The nurses moved toward the patients, saying, "Please stand back." I gave her a quick hug. Another nurse stood behind the desk and told about ten visitors, including me, "When I buzz the door, just leave." When the buzzer sounded we followed the instruction; the huge door swung open and we walked out. Then the buzzer sounded again and the doors closed behind us.

Day two and day three were the same as the first. I was told the doctors were trying different combinations of drugs to see what would work best for her. When I gave Mom her bath on the third day, I noticed the band that previously had been on her wrist was now on her left ankle. I was sure she had taken it off and then the nurses had placed it on her ankle because they assumed she would not find it there.

When I arrived on day four, Mom was standing at the nurses' station. She looked around, smiling, and said, "So, you finally came to get me. I have not seen you in a long, long time."

I said hello to everyone and asked her if she wanted to go to her room. We walked down the hall. Her name was still boldly written on the wall. I asked her who Barbara was. She looked at me and laughed. "You silly girl, that's me."

I had to talk her into taking a shower once again. When she was finished, I helped her dry her skin, then handed her the cream. She looked at me, somewhat confused. I took the cream, rubbed it in my hands, and then rubbed it on her back. I told her to do the same to her legs, hands, and tummy. She complied. Finally, she took a large amount of cream in her hands and rubbed it in her hair.

"It does not go in your hair," I told her.

She disagreed, "I've used this cream in my hair for a very long time." I did not fuss with her because for the first time since moving into the apartment, she seemed somewhat calm. I sat in front of the window and expected her to say she was going to jump out, but she did not. She only said, "I want to see my brother."

We sat and chatted for a bit. Again she put on extra clothing, and she also took lots of toilet paper and folded it into tiny neat squares and placed them in her bra. Over the past couple of days, I had left some additional items in her room and she was now wearing everything. When I tried to get the clothes off she resisted, so I just left them on her.

She again related how everyone at this house was so mean to her. "They are keeping me locked up and not letting me go home." She looked so fragile.

I felt so sorry for her because I knew what a kind, sweet, and wonderful person she used to be, and here she was calling people terrible names and clueless about the things coming out of her mouth. While we were chatting, someone walked by and she called him a name. "Please do not call people names because you will hurt their feelings, and I will not be around if they get angry at you and try to do something to you," I said.

"I don't care. He is a nigger, so what did I say that was wrong?"

I kept thinking how horrified Mom would be if she could only see herself. This disease extracts every ounce of dignity from its victims, one little piece at a time.

She asked to go for a walk, so we walked around the floor several times. On the way back, the night nurse said hello to Mom. "Hi," she replied, then muttered a curse word under her breath.

I apologized to the nurse. The nurse said it was nothing. "I have seen it all on this floor. What she said is tame compared to what other people say and try to do to me." I was embarrassed, but what could I do?

I took Mom back to her room. She said, "That nurse is a fucking bitch with a mop of dog hair on her head." The nurse had a full head of curly hair. I did not respond to her comments. As before, the bell rang and all the visitors were herded off the floor in a group.

On the seventh day of her stay, I received a call at work from the hospital telling me Mom would be discharged and I needed to be at the hospital by a certain time to have a discussion with the nurse about her continued care.

When I arrived, a nurse sat down with Mom and me to explain her medication and aftercare. Mom was given a month's supply of drugs. Going forward, she would have to be seen by a psychiatrist. Most of the medications were "hard drugs" and couldn't be prescribed by a family doctor. I was given a list of recommended psychiatrists to contact, and advised that if Mom began misbehaving, I must return her to the hospital immediately.

Mom did not participate in the conversation. She simply sat at the table playing with a cup and folding and unfolding a napkin. I told her we were going home. "Okay" was all I got from her. We returned to her room, I packed her belongings, and then we walked down the hallway to be buzzed out through the two huge doors.

Mom was a very different person compared to the one who had arrived at the hospital seven days earlier. She seemed a lot calmer, albeit a bit distant. The drugs seemed to have had a positive effect on her.

We walked down the second long hallway, took the elevator to the lobby, then exited to the parking lot. Mom wanted to know if we were going to see her mom and dad. I responded no, that we were going home.

As I drove away from the hospital, I wondered what type of life Mom would have being constantly medicated. I glanced in the rearview mirror and saw she was looking out the window, taking in all the new sights and sounds.

On the drive home, Mom remarked how there were so many houses and cars here and that she had never been here before. I simply agreed with her. This observation would be another recurring theme in the coming months.

HOME SWEET HOME

We arrived at the apartment as it was getting dark. I became anxious because I was not sure how Mom would react because of the "sundowning" problem.

I rang the bell. Ms. Muffin opened the door and we greeted each other. I helped Mom into the apartment. We sat on the couch and Mom looked around. "Is this where I live?" I said yes. "This is the first time I've been here."

I simply smiled. "Do you want something to eat?" Of course, the answer was yes. Now she would eat as much as anyone would give her. Even if she recently ate, she would tell you she had not eaten all day. It baffled me how her brain lacked the ability to tell her stomach she was full.

I sat watching Mom eat with a spoon and her fingers. She had completely forgotten how to use a fork, and using a spoon made things a lot less complicated. Mom had taken care of so many children and older people when she had worked, and here she was now, unable to eat her dinner properly.

When she was finished, she got up from the table, walked to the kitchen, and announced she was going to do the dishes. She proceeded to wash the dishes over and over again. She then wiped down the countertop and asked for the children. I told her the children were at home, but she insisted she had just seen them. "I have to make dinner for them." I told her we had already made dinner. She said that no one had informed her of that fact. I assured her it was fine and she needed to rest.

A few minutes later, Mom began the same conversation about the children and dinner. Prior to our taking her to the hospital, everyone was so afraid she would wake up in the middle of the night, come downstairs, and try to cook. We were hoping the medication would take away the desire to cook. It had not, although we were grateful for the other changes in her behavior.

About an hour after our arrival, Mom asked to go to the bathroom. She asked where it was and I pointed upstairs. I asked her if she needed me to go with her and she declined. She stayed in the bathroom for an extended period of time, which concerned me because I thought she was doing something she was not supposed to do. I finally went up the stairs and found her in the bathroom washing the hand towels. As soon as she saw me, she said, "It is dirty."

By now it was completely dark, and Mom was neither threatening anyone nor trying to run away. But later on that night, she tried to open the front door because she wanted to go outside. We decided the lock needed to be changed.

Mom kept going up and down the stairs searching for something. She would go up, go to the bathroom or her room, stay a few minutes, and come back down. She went up and down the stairs for a couple of hours. I told Ms. Muffin not to worry about the up and down—we had to trade off something, and she had improved a thousandfold from when they had first moved into the apartment.

When Mom finally sat down, she began talking about her brother and parents. She claimed to have just seen her parents and they both were fine. She spoke about her hometown as though she had just visited. After the conversation, she again said she had to go to the bathroom. She had forgotten she had gone less than half an hour before.

Upon returning from the bathroom, she announced it was dinnertime. I reminded her she had already eaten; she disagreed. I quickly changed the subject and dinner slipped out of her mind without her mentioning it again for the rest of the night.

It was now past 9:00. I told Ms. Muffin we should give Mom her sleeping pill, just in case it took a long time to take effect. She took it, and in the next twenty minutes or so, before it took full effect, she went to the kitchen four times and drank half a glass or more of water each time. She kept insisting she was thirsty. She then began to nod off, so Ms. Muffin took her upstairs and put her to bed. I silently prayed she would sleep through the night, all the time hoping the worst was behind us.

Ms. Muffin returned downstairs about fifteen minutes later and we spoke for a bit. She assured me she was going to do what was best for Mom and I should not worry. I was truly grateful for her care and concern.

It was late. I had a half-hour drive to get home, so I kissed Ms. Muffin good night and left.

On my way home my thoughts were racing. I was worried about Mom getting up during the night or sneaking out of the house. The what-if mantra played its warning drumbeat over and over in my head like a busted record. I have concluded that those two little words, "what if," are the saddest in the English language.

We are hoping her violent tendencies will disappear, but we will have to wait and see what happens. Medication is a new thing for all of us, and only time will tell.

MEDICATION

I never intended to put Mom on medication; however, I had no choice. In my opinion, as a nation we are drug-happy—and I am only talking about the legal ones. For everything that ails us, there seems to be a medication that can handle it. Even if you only suspect you have something, television commercials urge everyone to tell the doctor so they can get on that medication.

Having Mom on medication breaks my heart. Has her behavior improved? You bet it has, but at what cost? She is unsteady on her feet, slurs her words, shuffles when walking, and has the shakes. On the positive side, she is no longer violent. Not to mention, at sunset she does not want to go home and start World War II. She also sleeps most of the night now.

I had been at the apartment the night before. It had been a long day for me. The rain came down like it was celebrating Noah's boat and left water everywhere. I normally arrived at the apartment between 6:00 and 6:30 in the evening. Last night I got to the apartment at 8:40. It took me all of four hours to get there. By the time I got there, my nerves were shot.

Mom was already in her room. I heard her walking around. I went up the stairs just far enough to see her, but I didn't want her to see me. What I saw made me sadder than I am usually. There was Mom, staggering toward the door like she was drunk. She was drifting from side to side, holding on to the door and walls as she made her way to the bathroom. Once in the bathroom, she did what she had to do and flushed the toilet several times before reappearing and heading back to her room, staggering as she went. \

How can I not feel terrible when I see her this way? This is what I have done to her, to keep her under control.

Even though I know it is best for everyone that she is medicated, it is awful watching what the drugs have done to her and knowing I was the person who made the choice to medicate her.

THE WALKS

It was now mid-September. I asked Ms. Muffin and Cindy to take Mom for long walks on a daily basis. They readily agreed. We all would do whatever it took to keep Mom stable.

The walks were approximately one hour long. Prior to leaving for the walks, they made sure Mom went to the bathroom. The first few walks went off without any issues. A week or so into the routine, a half hour into the walk Mom asked to go to the bathroom. She was told they were not close to the house but turned around immediately and headed back to the apartment. Mom said she needed to go right away and just stood in the street and peed. When I heard about the incident, I instructed the ladies to keep Mom closer to the apartment.

I visited the apartment midweek and went for a walk with Mom. Before our walk Mom went to the bathroom. We walked along an industrialized section of the neighborhood where there is a storage facility in a large lot surrounded by trees and bushes. We were walking for about twenty minutes when Mom told me she had to go to the bathroom. I tried to explain to her that we needed twenty minutes to get back to the apartment. "I cannot wait," she said.

I turned around, took her hand, and began pulling her, just to try to make it back before she had an accident. She repeated, "I have to go." We were now in front of the storage facility, and I told her we could go around the facility so she could relive herself in the bushes. She refused, but I kept telling her I would be right there with her. We walked around the side of the building and I noticed a small clearing leading into a wooded area with several large bushes that gave some privacy from the passing traffic. I assured Mom it was safe to go there.

"I am afraid some little creature might crawl up my clothes once I begin to go," she said. I told her it was okay and assured her there were no creatures around. To my relief, she finally relented, stooped down, and peed.

After the bush foray, I figured we were in the clear and I walked her in the opposite direction, then turned to return to the apartment. Less than twenty-five minutes later, when we turned down the street toward the apartment, Mom once again announced it was time to go to the bathroom. Without thinking, I reminded her she had just urinated a little while ago.

"I did not!" she exclaimed.

"We will be home in a few minutes. Please wait until we get there." She got angry and began to curse and said she would not wait. "Give me a few minutes," I pleaded, once again pulling on her hand to make her walk faster.

However, she was in no mood to walk any faster than at her pace. She exclaimed, "I am going to pee!"

There was an open field to the right of us. I said, "Let's walk to the end of the field where there are several trees and you may be able to relieve yourself without anyone seeing you." We had walked only a few steps into the field when she began to undress. "You cannot undress in the street—this is a public place with people passing by!"

She made it clear she didn't give a fuck about people and what they thought. "I am a grown woman and can do whatever I want, and to fuck with everyone else." She simply stood there with her skirt pulled up almost over her head and peed. We walked back to the pavement to return to the apartment, and as she walked her shoes began making a wet, squishy sound because they were soaked. I had to make her take them off and drain them out. Once I got back to the apartment, I told Ms. Muffin, "We had an accident."

I made Mom take her shoes off outside before entering the apartment. Once inside, I walked her to the bathroom. Both she and the shoes took a bath that night. While Mom was taking a bath, I sat in the living room and cried. She no longer had the ability to understand anything, and I felt helpless because it did not matter what I did; I could not improve her memory or her life. I felt desperate.

THE WALKING CONTINUES

After the second peeing incident, I asked that Mom be taken on much shorter walks to avoid more accidents. I did not want her peeing on herself in public; this was just too much for me to handle. I am sure it was not good for her either.

The walks were now shorter, and everything seemed to be going well. It became a game: ten-minute walk, return home, urinate, rinse, and repeat. This went on for about a week until Mom made an announcement: "No more walks."

We needed to keep her on the go, so we decided to start a new game. She would be left alone for a couple of minutes, then someone would suggest going for a walk. If she refused, she was left by herself, then a couple of minutes later she would be asked again. If she refused, we would ask the same question, hoping she had forgotten and would agree to go. But if she kept refusing after ten minutes, we gave up.

It was a painstaking, exhausting task to deal with her. If we made a request and she did not want to do it, she would keep saying, "No, no, and no." If we tried to take her by the hand, she stood and literally dug her heels into the ground, refusing to move. We have considered changing the adage from "stubborn as a mule" to "stubborn as Mom" because she makes the mule seems a little more agreeable.

ADJUSTED ATTITUDE

Since leaving the hospital we've had to adjust Mom's medication twice. I am assuming this will be something that will happen quite often depending on her behavior.

Even though Mom is in a better place, she is still a handful. To give Ms. Muffin a break, I take Mom on Saturday. I try to keep her as occupied as possible. We go to church. The service is a bit long, three hours or more. Several times during the month we serve lunch.

During church, Mom sits looking somewhat lost, staring into space. If no one says anything to her, she simply sits there, almost like a fixture. When people approach her and ask if she remembers them, she smiles and says, "Who would forget such a lovely face? Of course I remember you, but your name escapes me."

Mom has known the head elder for many years. He is very involved in each service, but she no longer remembers him, and whenever she sees him she refers to him as the "fat minister."

One week when church was over and we went to the kitchen, I told her to sit down. I had to dish her food out for her because she could no longer accomplish this minor task. As soon as the food was given to her, she would immediately begin eating. When she was finished, I collected her plate.

After taking her plate away, I went to sit with her. A few minutes passed, and then she said, "I need to feel something under my teeth." This was her way of asking for something to eat. When I reminded her she had just ate, she denied it.

Mom has always had a sweet tooth; this has not changed. She is always asking for candy and cakes. If she refuses to go out, one of the surest ways of cajoling her is by promising her ice cream and cake. She is normally the first one out the door as soon as those words are mentioned. I try to keep her away from sugar, though, because we can see a significant negative behavioral change when she indulges in too much of it.

She has no idea what goes on in church. When we leave, she usually comments on how big the house is, referring to the church. It does not matter how many times you remind her it's the church.

A few months ago, we had a choir perform at church. It was a large choir visiting from the Bronx, New York. I took Mom to the kitchen with me before the service ended.

After lunch, the kids assisted with the dishes. There was a meeting shortly after lunch that the kids had to attend. There was still lots to be done in the kitchen when they left, so I asked Mom to help me because I had no one to sit with her. She loved to clean up and wash dishes.

I asked her to help wash the dishes. She poured out the dishwashing liquid and began to wash the dishes while I cleaned the stove and tables. While cleaning the tables, I noticed she was having a conversation with herself. I thought she needed something, so I walked over to her and asked if everything was all right. She kept repeating in a low voice, "Too many niggers."

"B, that is not nice," I told her.

It was like having a conversation with a brick wall. She didn't even acknowledge me. Once we left the church, she was her old self again.

Whenever we drive around, she always remarks that she has no idea how I find my way around, visiting all the "new" places we go.

DAY CARE

After a few months of attending day care, Mom began to recognize one of the streets going to the program. Twice per day she passed my house. By now she had long forgotten my house, but each day when she drove up the street I live on, she would say she must stop at my house because she didn't have any money and needed to get some change.

Mom started to recognize the street where the day care center was located. She kept telling everyone she did not wish to attend because there were too many old people there. She also said they made her work and never paid her, and she was tired of being a fool and working for nothing.

Each day, we made up a story to get her into the center. Once she got in the door and the workers called her by name, she would eagerly go to them, hugging and kissing them while keeping a close eye on the person who had escorted her from the car.

She was sometimes told the ladies had to go quickly and assist someone outside, and they would return shortly. While she was busy greeting the day care staff, the ladies would slip away and she was none the wiser.

As the long winter dragged on, she settled into her routine. It was, however, always difficult to get her out of the house. If the car did not come immediately, she would walk up and down the stairs, and at times she would take her clothes off.

Once she was up in the morning, she would have her breakfast and then her bath. Her clothes were always laid out for her, the closet door was locked, and only a few items were left in the chest of drawers. This prevented her from taking the clothes and hanging them all over the room. The medication had not taken this habit away.

146

To keep Mom from getting into mischief once she had her breakfast and was dressed, Ms. Muffin walked her to the end of the street and waited for Cindy's arrival. If Ms. Muffin did not do this, Mom would return upstairs, undress, and get back into her nightclothes.

It was a harsh winter that year; Mom had to be bundled up prior to going out. Once her coat and scarf were on, she would complain the coat was too heavy and she would start backing away from us because she didn't wish to put on anything else. Getting gloves on her hands was another ordeal. She had completely forgotten how to fit her fingers into them. We had to instruct her to hold her hands out, then try to put the gloves on. She would try to put several fingers into one finger in the glove, and when we told her this was incorrect she got annoyed and would begin sucking her teeth. After trying again and again with the gloves, Mom finally suggested cutting her fingers off to fit into the gloves. When we told her she had to be patient, she began to curse.

So we would remove the gloves, wait a few seconds, then say, "B, it's cold outside. May I help you put your gloves on?" Once again, we would ask her to hold her fingers out, then further instruct her to keep her fingers straight and extended. She did as instructed and we slipped on the gloves one finger at a time. That simple task took several minutes to accomplish.

MEDICATION CONTINUED

Each day I am grateful that Mom no longer wants to run away, but is there something out there that can tame her nasty tongue? I want to find a medication that can do that.

When we are driving in the car, she never wants me to stop, even at red lights. If I stop, she says, "Come on, let's fly!" If there is a car ahead of me, she will insultingly say, "Why is cock-tongue not moving?" When I try to explain that the light is red, she says, "Red means go." I will correct her that red means stop and green means go, but she does not believe me.

If someone cuts me off in traffic, she talks about getting a gun and shooting him in the crotch. "What is that ass doing? Does he want to kill us?" She refers to many drivers as "cockheads." She has a filthy mouth, and she talks badly about everyone. She calls me an ass, Sally is a bitch, Amy is a hard-foot bitch—no matter who you are, you are not spared from her tongue.

She has something nasty to say about everyone behind their back. When she makes comments to me about others, it makes me very upset. I want to have a glimpse of the person she was not so long ago. Where is that person hiding?

The medications are working, but they have horrible side effects. When we go for walks now, they are much shorter. I have to hold her hand to avoid her stumbling. We continue to tinker with the medication. When an old habit that we thought went away surfaces, I call the doctor and dosages are changed to counteract what is going on. Each time I call the doctor's office, I feel sick and can't help but cry. Perhaps one of these days I will get used to her being on medication.

In my ideal world she would not have to take any medication because I believe they do more harm to the body than good, but we are not living in an ideal world. I know if she were not on the medication, there would be no controlling her.

THE SEWING MACHINE

My maternal grandmother was born in 1905. She was always such a strong and remarkable woman. She could neither read nor write, but she was the most astute person I encountered as a child. She had so much knowledge. As far as I was concerned, she knew everything. If someone was sick, she knew exactly which herbal remedy to give to make that person better. If a baby had a problem with his or her eye or tummy, she knew how to make the baby well.

She worked very hard taking care of everyone and knew exactly what to do no matter what was going on. She could cook, bake, and sew; she planted her own kitchen and flower gardens.

Growing up, we had no electricity or running water. My grandmother taught us everything girls had to know. Growing up in the '60s was quite different, and girls had to learn certain things to make them "nice ladies." I learned how to cook and sew at an early age. I was about six when I learned to sew and eight when I learned how to cook. Grandma sewed by hand with a needle and thread. When I was around eight, she finally got a sewing machine that operated by hand. It was a small Singer machine that had a little handle; you would turn the handle with your right hand and guide the fabric with your left hand. I preferred sewing with the needle and thread because I could handle it much better than the little machine.

She sewed most of our clothing, and whenever anyone in the family became pregnant, she made all the clothes for the baby. There was cotton fabric and colored thread in a box, and Grandma would cut the little gowns out and we would put them together. All the gowns she made had a small hand-embroidered section in the front. They were beautiful. She had an array of stitches she used for the gowns—to this day I still remember some of those stitches.

In the summer of 2014, my husband and I visited a museum in New Jersey that featured some garments from the early twentieth century. I saw one of the garments and recognized several of the stitches, and there I was explaining to my husband how these stitches were done because I had learned them from my grandmother.

Mom had long forgotten how to sew with a sewing machine—or, for that matter, by hand. A few weeks ago, I took her to visit an old friend of the family. When we arrived, our friend had two other visitors. One of the visitors was assisting in the kitchen while the other was sewing some curtains. When we entered the bedroom, I told Mom to sit down and she did, but she did not sit in the place I had told her to sit; instead, she sat down very close to the visitor who was sewing and stared curiously at what she was doing. She seemed to be lost in the moment.

I had to call Mom's name several times before getting a response. "What are you doing?" I asked.

She responded by saying she was just watching. She continued staring at the lady sewing for about thirty minutes or more, never moving her eyes from the sewing machine.

I assumed that, someplace in her mind, she must have recognized the machine and perhaps realized that she should know how to sew too.

ANIMALS ON PARADE

Mom and I visited an old friend. We stayed with her for about an hour. I always feel so bad when people see Mom and they have such sad expressions on their faces. They always say, "She used to be so nice." Visiting this friend was no different. She repeated what I have heard so many times in the past few years. Our friend is almost twenty years older than Mom and is still in pretty good shape at her age.

Once the visit was over, I decided not to take the highway home because I was tired of watching the sound barriers and listening to Mom say the same thing over and over again. So instead of turning left, we turned right and drove through a residential neighborhood. We were, therefore, forced to drive at a much slower speed than we would have on the highway. At this speed Mom was able to see lots of houses and people. She had a running commentary about each person she saw.

The first few people she saw, she commented on how this person looked like a family member of hers, that person looked like her sister, the other person was her niece, etc. But finally, when there were no more family members for comparison, her comments became more cynical. She noticed a man on the sidewalk and said that his nose resembled that of a donkey she knew. Farther down the street, we saw a short lady with a prominent chest, and Mom commented that her breasts were so large, she must be nursing a horse. Another person was ugly, another person was fat, the other person looked like a pig, someone else looked like a monkey, someone else looked like a cow, another one was a jackass—it simply went on and on.

Many years ago I called an actress ugly. Mom was very disappointed that I could say something like that. She told me God did not make anything ugly. I told her as far as I was concerned, the actress was ugly. Now that she is ill, she is the one calling many people ugly. Why? Who knows?

FOLDING CLOTHES

There was a time when Mom folded clothes like a professional. Not a single crease could be seen when she was finished. She even color-coordinated the clothes in neat piles. I guess this habit went back to the days when she had been a maid and had to do a perfect job for her clients.

We had a get-together at Mom's house, and when we got there Ms. Muffin was still doing the laundry. She asked Mom to accompany her to the basement to assist in folding the clothes. I decided to go with them.

Ms. Muffin carefully removed the clothes from the dryer a few pieces at a time and handed a pile to Mom. She sat down and looked at the pile for a little while, then began putting one piece of clothing into the other. She could not figure out what to do. When the folding didn't work as Mom had envisioned, she asked Ms. Muffin to show her how it was done. She had now totally forgotten how to fold clothes.

OLD MAN WINTER

The winter of 2013–2014 was brutal. I thought the winter would keep summer at bay forever. It just kept snowing. New snow met the old snow on the ground. It snowed every week, or so it seemed. It reminded me of the winters from the '80s when the snow never seemed to stop. This weather mirrored my mood: cold, gray, and sad.

I have been watching helplessly as Mom sinks deeper into this disease. I no longer ask why because there is no point.

My sleep pattern is off. I was a terrible sleeper as a child. Once I became an adult I began sleeping a little better. However, once we finally knew Mom was sick, I went back to my non-sleeping self. Now I go to bed and am up in a couple of hours. Once awake, my mind begins racing, thinking about all the things I have to do for her. No matter what I do, I cannot seem to stop my mind from wandering all over the place. I am unable to control my thoughts. My brain does exactly what it wants to do and I am powerless to stop it.

All these sleepless nights are such a drag. I have terrible headaches. I am not sure if the headaches come because I am sleep-deprived or if there is something else going on. I do not want to go to the doctor because I am afraid of what he might tell me. If I go and he sends me for a scan and there is something going on in my head, then I am not sure how I will be able to live with myself knowing that I have brain issues. I certainly do not want to become like Mom, so I have decided I will learn how to live with my headaches because I do not wish to know the truth about what is actually going on.

WINDOWS

I went for my usual midweek visit to see Mom. When I arrived, the apartment was quite cold, which was odd because the heat was turned up very high. We try to keep the place warm because Mom seems to get the shivers a lot lately. I am assuming her shivers are one of the many side effects of her medication.

I walked through the apartment and could not find the source of the coldness; there was no draft coming through the door, so I decided to examine the windows. I went through the first floor and all the windows were tightly shut. Finally, I went upstairs to Mom's room. When I pulled up the shades, I found the answer to Jack Frost's visit.

Somehow Mom had figured out how to open the windows. She had opened both windows in her room just a few inches wide. Once this was done, she had lowered the shades. With the shades closed, I would never have guessed that winter was creeping in through her window.

WINDOW BLINDS

Mom's apartment, like my home, has shades on each window. I began noticing there were small sections of the shades missing. At my house, the bottom section of the shade was missing, along with two slats. The slats were placed on the window ledge; the rest of the shade was intact, with the exception of the missing sections.

When I went to the apartment, I noticed the same thing. Most of the window shades had a few slats missing.

It seemed Mom had carefully removed sections of the shade along with a couple of slats without causing any damage to the entire shade. The wand and pulleys to operate the shade were in good working order and the cord loops were not disturbed; with the exception of the missing slats, everything was working. I have no idea how she accomplished this task.

THE STORE

When we were young, I never remembered going shopping with Mom. We were so poor that my memory of shopping was not shopping at all. The church we attended in the mid- to late '70s had a basement of donated clothing. On Saturday nights, we used to go there, and the lady who was overseeing the basement store would say to us kids, "Take whatever can fit you." That was my memory of shopping with Mom.

When I go shopping now and see mothers with their children, I feel a little cheated because I never had this opportunity with Mom. I know this may seem insignificant to some, but memories are what make us who we are, and I have a few pieces that are missing.

Now that Mom is ill, she loves to go to the store. When she enters most stores, she thinks she is working there. If something is on the floor, she picks it up, puts it back on the hanger, and returns it to the rack. She then looks at the prettiest dresses on the rack. When there are beautiful dresses, she will walk from rack to rack telling me which ones she wants. She hands them to me or Ms. Muffin, and as soon as she walks to the next rack, we usually return the dress to the rack. This can go on for several hours. Finally, we exit the store without buying anything and she does not remember she wanted the beautiful dresses.

If we visit a store and she does not like anything, she will let us know that it is time to leave. If we linger, she will tell us, "Let's leave now." If we do not move along as quickly as she thinks we should, she will keep shaking her hands and stomping her feet, insisting it is time to leave—and leave we must, because if we don't she will get angry and stay angry for a long time.

NOT MY HOUSE

Even on medication, as night approaches Mom still has that nervous tension and still paces, going up and down the stairs and looking through the windows. She can go up and down the stairs one hundred times.

A few months ago, we were at my house just as it was beginning to get dark. She began telling me we had to leave because the owner of the house would be returning, and if she found us at the house she would be very angry. "The lady left a few weeks ago and did not leave any money for me. I feel like an ass because I am working and not getting paid. I don't know why I am so stupid."

When I attempted to reassure her that no one was coming and the house was mine, the situation worsened. She walked out the back door, sat down on the back stairs, and started begging me to leave. She began rubbing her hands together and kept looking behind her as though she was looking for someone. She was so anxious, and no matter what I told her, she just got more nervous.

I repeated that the house was mine and no boss was coming. "Even if you have papers showing you own this house, my boss is returning, and this is her house, so we must leave."

There was nothing I could do to calm her down. She just kept going on and on about her boss. I finally took her home. Once we were in the car, she calmed down.

THE FAT CAT

I own a cat that is really fat. I adopted him as an adult and he came already weighing in at twenty-seven pounds. He is very independent and not very people-oriented, especially around strangers. However, with Mom he is the sweetest cat ever.

As a rule, he does not allow anyone to touch his belly. Whenever Mom visits, as soon as he hears her voice, he comes right over and sits very close to her. If she is standing, he circles her legs while brushing up next to her. He rubs his head on her legs and meows up at her. She can scratch and touch him wherever she wishes and he does not resist. I think he may have some sort of sixth sense that tells him she is ill, and because he knows she is ill, she is allowed to do whatever she wants with him. He will allow her to rub and scratch him for the longest time. I find that quite interesting. He has never allowed me to do this to him.

Mom no longer remembers his name. She knows he is a cat, so she renamed him Meow-Meow. She always wants to know if "she" (the cat) has a boyfriend. I always remind her he is a male cat, but that does not register in her head. Whatever Mom eats, somehow ends up on the floor for him, although I repeatedly tell her he does not eat people food. It runs the gamut: fruit, meat, bread, dessert, salads—eventually she will pass whatever she is eating on to him.

I left her alone in the kitchen a few weeks ago. When I returned, her plate was on the floor and she had poured her orange juice in the plate and given it to the cat. He was sitting not too far away from her, and she could not understand why he was not drinking his milk.

THE FAT CAT II

During one of our long drives the other day, Mom wanted to know how Meow-Meow was doing. She told me he was at home waiting for his paycheck. When I asked why he was getting a paycheck, she said he had worked very hard and we needed to pay him. She then asked if I knew there were two cats. "I saw both of them. One bought a shirt, and I saw him place the shirt on Meow-Meow, and he was happy to get his new shirt."

I had no idea that my cat wore shirts.

THE ABSENCE OF AN ULCER

Like her brother who is also ill, Mom suffers from ulcers. She has had an ulcer for over forty years and had been hospitalized twice due to complications from the ulcer, both times for a week or more because it was bleeding.

She used to live on a restricted diet. There were so many things she could not eat or drink because it would irritate her condition. When she was well, she would frequently tell me her stomach was bothering her. For years she took over-the-counter medication to control the acid in her stomach. She also took alternative medications to assist her with the pain. Certain activities she could not do because they aggravated her condition.

Currently, she does not remember anything about her ulcer. She has not mentioned it for years. Lately, she will eat whatever we put in front of her. If the ulcer is bothering her, we have no way of knowing. She still steals food if it is left unattended. If the food is spicy she will eat it, and even then no mention of her ulcer. I find it quite interesting that she does not complain. This is something that plagued her for almost half her life, and now, like so many things, it has disappeared.

HER HAIR

There was a time when Mom had beautiful long hair. As she got older, her hair became shorter and shorter. Since her illness began, I have kept it very short and cropped close to her head.

These days everything seems to end up in her hair. If she is moisturizing her body, the moisturizing cream will eventually end up in her hair. If she gets her hand on any type of oil or soap, that ends up in her hair too.

The other day, her hair felt brittle and hard. We were trying to figure out what she had come in contact with to put in her hair. We do not keep gel handy, so this was ruled out. The following day we were still trying to figure out what had happened and discovered, quite by accident, that it was toothpaste! She had found the tube in the bathroom and just put the toothpaste in her hair.

I can certainly understand her missing her mouth when brushing her teeth, but in her hair? Who puts toothpaste in their hair?

THE PEACOCK

As Mom's disease has progressed, she has also become very interested in men and sex. She will flirt with most men she meets. However, if the man is old, she wants nothing to do with him.

Prior to Mom's illness, with the exception of our father, I was aware of Mom having had only one boyfriend.

She began dating him just before I went to college. When we were much younger, she always told us she didn't want a man who would treat us badly, so she did not date. Other than work and church, Mom had no social life. She always held two jobs. Saturday was Sabbath, so nothing could be done on that day—from sunset on Friday to sunset on Saturday.

Mom dated her boyfriend for about four years. Just before I graduated college, she informed me they had broken up because he was cheating on her and had gotten a young lady pregnant and had to marry her.

When she found out about the affair, she was crushed. I knew she wanted to marry him. While she was telling me about the affair, she said she believed he was not in love with her but was secretly in love with me. According to her, he always seemed more interested in me and how I was doing even before I went away to college. She even told me the girl he was seeing was my age, and that proved he was not in love with her. I told her she should not think that way. I tried to tell her that he had never said or done anything that would lead me to think he was interested in me. After the breakup, she never dated anyone else that I knew about.

After that experience she got a little bitter and angry at the world, but who could blame her? She deserved some kind of happiness, but it never really came.

Now in her illness, I guess in some part of her head, she thinks she can find the man of her dreams.

When Mom gets dressed she stands in front of the mirror, strokes her face, brushes her hair back with her fingers, and admires herself. She turns around, examining herself, while fixing her clothes.

If her clothing is a little loose, she uses a belt or something else to make the clothes fit tighter. Everything she has on now has to be close-fitting. She has sweaters that are slightly larger than normal, and she will pull the fabric at the front and tie the extra fabric into a knot. If she has a dress on that is a little big, she uses a belt to tighten it around her waist. She walks around like a peacock, displaying all her feathers for the world to see. She does not see the person we see. We are assuming she is seeing herself as a young person and that her brain has fooled her into thinking she is much younger than she actually is.

She began telling us she needed a man and described to us in graphic detail what she needed. In her description, she pounds her fists on the table as an illustration. Some of the things she says make me blush. Mom was never like this. In her current state, she no longer has a filter; everything just tumbles out, no matter how crude.

Lately, I've been thinking perhaps she had all of these things hidden in her mind all these years, and now that she is ill and is filter-less they just come out. Was she always like this and I did not know? Was she that good at hiding her true self that I never noticed it before? Who is this stranger who says the dirtiest things? This is certainly not the Mom I know. Is this just her illness or something else?

Was Mom so deprived of love and affection that now, in her illness, everything just comes flooding out, no matter how crude? Her language and behavior are really embarrassing.

165

THE FISH IN THE SKY

I must confess I am a workaholic. I am always at work; I seldom take time off. I have too many bills and way too much responsibility to just sit at home and do nothing.

It's a financial drain caring for Mom; I never imagined I would have full financial responsibility for her. I assumed once she got older and needed care, all of her children would pool our money to care for her. I was mistaken.

When the subject came up initially about who would care for her, I was told by one of my siblings to turn her over to the state and let them take care of her. I could never turn her over to the state. If I did that, I would not be able to live with myself; I probably would just shrivel up and die. So I decided it is better for me to mortgage my future and provide for her now rather than let her go to some God-forsaken nursing home.

A few weeks ago, I needed to take a day off to run some errands. I told Ms. Muffin I would pick Mom up from day care. I had to visit an old friend and took Mom along for the ride. Mom and this lady had been friends for over forty years. However, Mom did not remember her, although she pretended that she did. And that was another thing—how did she know she was supposed to pretend? At times she was such a good actress.

On the way to our friend's house, there is a small airport just off the highway. As we drove past the airport, an incoming airplane flew over in preparation for its landing. Mom looked over and told me, "Look, there is a fish to fry!"

Without thinking, I asked, "Where is the fish?"

She told me it was flying in the sky and pointed up at the plane as it flew by.

THE LAMPS

In the apartment where Mom lives there are no overhead lights in the bedrooms. Instead, we have two lovely lamps neatly placed on the nightstand on either side of her bed. The lamps were untouched and worked well for a few days. About a week after the lamps were placed in the room, Mom came home one day from day care and disappeared into her room for a couple of hours. Everyone was happy because she was not being disruptive. No one went upstairs to check on her. We all assumed she was taking a nap.

She finally emerged for dinner. Afterward she went upstairs and had a bath. When Ms. Muffin took Mom into her room to get her ready for bed, she discovered why Mom was so quiet. She had carefully disassembled both lamps.

The shades were carefully separated from the lamp and sat on the far side of the room. The switches were removed along with the bases. Even the wires running through the lamps were disconnected. Everything had been carefully and painstakingly taken apart and left in neat little piles on the floor.

MOVING DAY

We eventually moved Mom and Ms. Muffin out of the apartment and back to the house we had bought for her. Sally and her husband bought a house across the street from Mom's and moved out. The Sunday before the official move, we started taking small items to the house from the apartment. We were doing the move ourselves, so we did anything we could to lighten the major load on moving day.

We moved most of the food items. We packed everything in the cupboards at the house. We were on our third trip and had just finished putting some dishes away when, being somewhat tired, Ms. Muffin and I forgot to lock the door that now separated the kitchen and dining room. For a few seconds, we lost track of Mom. We were both in the living room talking when I heard the audible click of the stove. I ran to the kitchen and found Mom at the stove; she had turned the burner on. I rushed toward her, grabbed her by the hand, and told her we were not going to cook.

She yanked her hand away and angrily asked if I was afraid she would burn the house down. I was afraid she would burn herself because the concept of heat was now foreign to her. I told her that we had already cooked. She stomped out of the kitchen muttering, "Never mind."

Moving is not easy, but moving with someone who cannot remember much is an ordeal.

We moved Mom and Ms. Muffin back to the house on Memorial Day 2014. It struck me as being peculiar—not peculiar funny, but peculiar strange, that we had chosen this day to move.

Memorial Day was earmarked to recall all the heroes who protected and gave their lives for our country. But it also struck me that memorial means remembrance. To remember is a great thing, but for Mom it is a privilege she lacks. The general public takes remembering for granted.

For Mom, that part of her life was over. She had no idea she was moving back to her home. She had always loved to travel. She did it all her life, and here she was, perhaps making the final move of her life—and she had no clue what was going on.

For the big move we rented a U-Haul, which Stephen drove. My brother-in-law had his SUV, Sally had her car, Cindy had another car, and I had my own car. For the first trip, we had Mom sit in my car with Ms. Muffin for the short ride over. Once we arrived, we told Ms. Muffin to sit outside with Mom so she would not get in the way. Once everything was unloaded, we decided to let Mom and Ms. Muffin sit in the house. This way, Mom would be safely out of the way for the time being.

When we returned on the second trip, Mom came out of the house and stood on the sidewalk in everyone's way. When I asked her to move so we could begin unloading the vans and cars, she refused. Knowing she would listen to Stephen, I asked him to speak to her and move her along; as soon as he asked, she listened.

We finally got her into the house and allowed her to do one thing to keep her occupied: She was allowed to move a tiny bag with some clothes in it. The bag kept her occupied for a long time, and that was good for all of us.

Lunchtime rolled around and I warmed up some food we had prepared previously. She ate and, true to form, a few minutes later said she was hungry. By that point, I was no longer telling her she had just ate. What was the point? I gave her a fruit, she ate it, and again she told me she was hungry. Sally told me she was going for ice cream and wanted to know if she could get one for Mom. I told her no. Sally then suggested an Italian ice instead; I agreed.

Several minutes later Mom again complained about being hungry, so I gave her a cup of tea. She took a sip and handed it back to me, saying, "It is not sweet, make it sweet." I added honey until the tea was sweet enough for her.

By the time Sally returned with the ice cream and Italian ice, Mom was still drinking her tea. Tara handed Mom the little cup of Italian ice. Mom dropped several scoops into her tea and continued drinking. Tara was about to say something, and I silently gestured with my fingers to my lips. What sense was there in telling her that blue Italian ice did not belong in her tea? Lately, unless it is something that could be harmful to her, whatever she did with her food was fine with me.

Less than two minutes later, Mom was pouring her tea into the container with the rest of the Italian ice. Sally noticed and told Mom not to do it, but I told Sally not to bother her.

If you fuss with her, she gets angry, and once she is angry it lasts way too long, as far as I am concerned. I've decided we do not need the aggravation. It is too exhausting to have to deal with the same thing over and over again.

THE SETUP

The entire move took about six hours. Because we were going only ten minutes away, we thought it would take less time.

I placed Mom's clothes in her closet, but not the closet she initially had when she lived in the house. We moved her into the room just across from the bathroom; we did not want her getting lost at night trying to find it.

We were planning to install a lock on the closet door but ran out of time. I told Ms. Muffin that perhaps, because everything was new, Mom would not be able to find the closet, and even if she did I was sure it would take a while. As it turned out, it did not take long. Before dinner was served, she was already going through the closet. She removed some of her dresses, shoes, and whatever else she could find. She began twisting buttons off dresses and coats, and also tried to remove stitches from seams. I could not believe it.

After dinner she took a bath, changed into her nightclothes, then went into the closet, removed a dress, and put it on over her nightclothes. Then she came downstairs and sat down to watch TV.

Ms. Muffin and I went to Mom's room and placed a small chest of drawers in front of the closet door, hoping it would stop her from going into the closet. A few minutes later, Mom went upstairs and moved the chest of drawers so carefully that none of us downstairs heard her. When we went upstairs, we found her sitting on the bed with the entire contents of the chest on her bed and the closet door wide open, with some of the items on the floor. She had also changed her clothing; now she had two dresses on and a pair of shoes that did not match.

As usual, she was able to do whatever she wanted and quickly removed whatever barriers we put in her way. It had taken her no time at all to find where the closet was. Any door to her, is a way to get to the great unknown. I had no choice but to lock the closet door. In the next couple of weeks, we had to start locking all the doors in the house.

NEW TEETH

For as long as I can remember, Mom has worn partial dentures. On the top of her mouth she is missing her front teeth and two molars; on the bottom she is missing several molars.

In early 2014, a tooth cracked and a small portion broke off. Without that tooth, her top partials do not fit properly. I tried to make an appointment to take her to the dentist, but she refused to go. I reminded her a week or so later that we needed to do something about her tooth. Since she did not respond, I took this as consent to set up the appointment. When the day arrived, I picked her up but did not tell her she was going to see the dentist because I am sure she would have declined.

It took a total of four visits to have the problem tooth fixed. Now she has a new cap on the tooth and it looks great.

This little episode brings me to another interesting question: How does Mom remember, on her own, to remove her partials and clean them? After each meal she goes to the bathroom, removes the partials and washes them, rinses her mouth, and returns the partials to her mouth. How can her brain remember this?

The dentist told us that Mom's top partials needed to be replaced. Once I got the money together, the work began. It took several visits to the dentist before the partials were ready. Finally, it was time to get her new teeth.

The teeth were expertly fitted, adjusted, tweaked, flipped, flopped, and buffed. After all the modifications were completed, the final fitting was done. Mom finally said they fitted fine.

We arrived home after the dentist appointment and dinner was served. Mom then watched a little television and went up to the bathroom. Later on, she had a supervised bath. There was a little pile of toilet paper left after her bath, and Ms. Muffin was in the process of getting rid of the paper when she noticed one crumpled bundle seemed heavier than the others.

She carefully unfolded the paper, and there were Mom's new teeth. We assumed they were uncomfortable because she had never done anything like this previously.

We notified the dentist and took the teeth back for more adjustments. Two weeks after Mom got her teeth, we were at the table having lunch when Mom said something. I looked over at her and it occurred to me that her new cap tooth was missing.

We had no idea what happened to it; it was never found, so we were not sure if she had swallowed it. I decided I was not going to replace it; I saw no point to it.

WHO ARE YOU?

Each time Mom gets her medication, my heart sinks. Sometimes I feel so sad for her, but if I have to tell the truth, I feel very sad for myself and my siblings because of the mystery of the disease. The "great unknown" is how I describe this disease, because of the lack of knowledge and the fact that nothing can be done to slow down or stop it once it manifests itself.

I am unsure what depression is; however, lately I think I may be depressed. It is difficult to explain how I feel. To really understand how I feel, you would have to be in a similar situation. It's impossible to put into words exactly how I am feeling—a combination of grief, loss, and utter desperation.

I grieve because Mom is no longer with us. She is alive but missing in action. However, the person who is alive is no longer Mom. Mom, as I knew her, died several years ago, and now we have this stranger who somehow looks like Mom but is not really her. Rather, she is someone who came in unannounced and has taken full control of the person Mom used to be. It's like the premise of the old movie *Invasion of the Body Snatchers*. She has the same face and the same body but is a totally different person.

The person who Mom was is so different from this new person that, even after all these years, I still have not sorted out what is really going on. Currently I am trying to figure out if I ever really knew Mom at all. I question everything about the person she used to be. I wonder if Mom was so good at acting that she hid this current version of herself out of sight from us for so many years, and now that she is no longer in control, the real her is the person we now know. I do not know what to think or believe.

Once belief is gone, what's left? I always admired the person Mom was. She worked so hard. She was so unselfish and kind. I am so confused. I don't know what I should believe about her. Several months ago, I called Sally because I wanted her to confirm that I had not fabricated how nice Mom was. Perhaps I had forgotten and maybe I was making it all up in my head? She told me Mom was nice. This entire situation is slowing driving me nuts!

Gone now are the days when she cried for anything and everything. Back then she drove me up the wall when she cried, but, my God, how I long for those days to return. A tiny hint of the Mom that used to be would be greatly appreciated. Just a little hint, a little spark of those days gone by—I don't think that is such a strange request.

If there truly is a God, and these days I wonder if He really does exist, how could He allow this to happen? What good could ever come out of something this awful? The Bible states that "all trials are for the good of God's children." I now beg to differ; I am at a total loss to see what good could ever come out of this.

She is lost to the world, lost to herself, and totally lost to everyone else. The sun of this life has set on her. She has breath in her body and life in her veins because her heart is pumping blood throughout her body, but she is dead. This disease has taken her life. Life is lost when the brain no longer functions. She is now gone, never to return.

LUNCH AWAY FROM HOME

Mom and I attended church the Saturday before Easter 2014. Lunch was served that day, and I was still in charge of the kitchen. Therefore, before the midday service began, I went to the kitchen to put the food in the oven. I took Mom with me. She sat down at one of the tables, got a book that someone had left behind, and started reading aloud.

I gave her some grapes to keep her quiet while I concentrated on putting the food in the oven. She kept reading and eating the grapes. About ten minutes later, she got bored, got up, and asked if she could help me. I told her she could wipe the tables. I handed her a wet sponge and she wiped and wiped the tables.

She cleaned the tables for fifteen minutes, then said she was hungry. I gave her another snack, some soup with a small slice of bread. Fifteen minutes later, lunch was served and I gave her lunch.

She finished her meal and called me. When I looked at her, she said in a somewhat low tone, while pointing to her plate, "I am hungry."

"You just finished eating."

"I did not eat." Mom again pointed to her plate. "Come and give me something to eat."

Some of the ladies at the table began to smile. I walked over and gave Mom another bowl of soup. She drank it and then called me again, asking for more food.

At this point she had already eaten too much. Mom was now getting upset because I would not give her more food. One of the ladies sitting next to her got up and came over to ask how much Mom had eaten. I looked at Mom, and she was in the process of moving the lady's plate in front of her. The other ladies at the table had to move the plate away from her.

When Mom saw there was no more food coming, she got up with the bowl and came to the kitchen, wanting to wash the dish. It was a disposable bowl, so washing it was unnecessary. She insisted on washing the bowl, though, and went over to the sink to do exactly that.

She took the washed bowl back to the table and simply sat there. She was so upset at me because she did not get any additional food.

I called out to her a couple of times, but she refused to acknowledge me. The third time I called her, she leaned over and told the lady next to her that I was a pain in the ass. She remained angry for the rest of the afternoon.

I don't understand how she remembers to be angry.

LUNCH

Over the past few weeks I've become extremely emotional. I want to be able to hold on to some kind of hope, no matter how small it may be, that somehow I will be able to help Mom get better. I'm afraid if I give up hope, I will just shrivel up and die, so I keep hoping, knowing full well that nothing will change.

Sometimes I feel like screaming at the top of my lungs. Lately, I am wondering how long I can cry before I run out of tears. I am tired of crying. I wanted to give her a better life, but that was stolen from me. Is it wrong to want something better for her? She never got the opportunity to have the life she wanted; is it so wrong to want her to have a good ending? I don't see a problem with that, but the unkindness continues for her. She will end her life in total confusion, and I am having a difficult time coming to terms with this. Why did she have to get this sick? She should be allowed to end her life with some dignity and peace. Our reality now is different, though; I know bad things happen to good people, but why her?

My sad moods are back. They come now without warning. The sadness is so overwhelming I am unable to shake it.

One day Mom and I went to church. Afterward, I didn't feel like going home to watch Mom go up and down the stairs, asking for the location of the bathroom or for her mom and dad, so I invited one of my fellow church members out to lunch.

We went to an Indian restaurant. On Saturday they served lunch buffet style, so this made it much easier for me. I sat Mom down and dished out her lunch: soup in a bowl, salad in another bowl, and her lunch on a plate.

Mom was already digging in when I returned to the table with my lunch. She ate her meal, then poured her soup over her salad and ate it.

Our church colleague and I were talking when Mom announced she was finished and began cleaning the table. "I am going to wash the dishes," she said. I explained to her we were not at home and she would not be allowed to wash the dishes. I pointed out the waitresses and told her they would be doing the dishes.

Mom simply ignored me. She got up and headed across the restaurant. I had to get up and run after her as she made her way toward the kitchen. I stepped into her path and reminded her we were not at home as she glared and cursed me. "Get out of my fucking way! I am going to the kitchen, and you can't stop me from washing the dishes." I did not move and she tried to push me out of her way.

The owner of the restaurant came over to find out what was going on. I told her Mom was behaving badly because she was ill. When Mom saw she would not be allowed to go into the kitchen, she turned and headed for the exit. I told the owner I needed the bill and motioned to my friend to stand next to the exit. When he did, Mom moved to the side of the door and just stood there looking out of the huge glass windows. The other people in the restaurant must have thought we were totally crazy. I was running after Mom from the back to the front of the restaurant. I went to the window and tried to talk to her, but she refused to answer me. The bill was handed to me and I paid quickly. Lunch was over.

We walked to the car and I put Mom in the backseat. Then I reversed the car out of the parking space. As we were driving through the parking lot, she simply opened the car door. I just felt a rush of wind. "What is that?" I guess I must have screamed because I heard the back door slam shut.

This incident really terrified me. I knew I hadn't buckled her seatbelt because she was so enraged and did not want me to touch her.

The only thing I could say to my friend was "God takes care of fools and children, she being the latter and I the former."

I am sure that if someone had pricked me with a pin after the door slammed shut, not one drop of blood would have flowed. I was so scared that I began to shake.

How could she open the door while I was driving? She had totally forgotten how dangerous her actions were.

SPRING

It is spring 2014 and Mom's memory continues to deteriorate. That may sound a little strange, given that she has memory issues. In the past couple of months, she has lost her ability to carry on a normal conversation. She will start to say something and then, before she can complete the thought, she will start on another unrelated topic. Now whatever she says I just agree with, and at times I say "I know" or something just as nonsensical. She does not know the difference, no matter what is said.

She will start saying something, then get frustrated and tell me she has trouble remembering. We were talking recently. She started saying something, and halfway through she suddenly stopped and said she could not remember what she wanted to say.

She said, "You know, I have a big brain, but whenever I want to say something, my brain goes *whoosh*." As she spoke, she illustrated with her hands, starting with her hands apart to signify a big brain, then bringing them back together to imitate a small space for the "whoosh" part. That was what happened when I tried to say something.

I looked at her and told her a bold-faced lie: that there was nothing wrong with her brain: "Not to worry about forgetting things. You are all right."

I often wonder if she remembers that she is forgetting, and if she does, does that make her scared?

WISHING AND HOPING

It's now the end June 2014, and for the past two weeks Mom has been in a good mood. This makes me very happy. Her world, to me, expands. Although she can no longer explain what she feels in her head, I assume she is not anxious when this mood surfaces.

She still manages to pray. However, at times her prayers will wander off into other subjects, but if we ask her to pray, she tries. We keep wishing and hoping her mood will stabilize and she can be as happy as this disease will permit.

I don't know what I can do for her other than keep her clean, feed her, and provide living comforts. I truly wish there was something else that could be done.

I pray for God's grace to shine on her and that she can continue to be in this good mood, even though each day she is losing another part of herself. I still pray that someday her mind will be unshackled and once again she will become her old self—the old self that now is truly out of sight. For her the windows are closed, the shades drawn, and the lights permanently off.

I want to be able to sit and talk with her and for her to remember that I came to see her. I want her to remember when I leave. I want her to know that she is loved and appreciated. I want her to know that her life still has meaning, perhaps not to the world but to the children she has worked and cared for. I want her to know that she has made a difference in people's lives. She adds meaning and substance to the lives of others.

Ms. Muffin took her food shopping in one of those megastores the other day, and a man came over and said to mother, "Is your name Barbara?" Mom, of course, did not respond. Ms. Muffin told the man Mom was ill. He stood there for some time telling

Ms. Muffin how Mom had changed his life. Apparently, he had met Mom when she was working at the day care center. He had a couple of children from a previous marriage and at the time had wanted to date a young lady he knew, but he had no one to babysit his children. Mom volunteered and kept babysitting at no charge until he married the young lady. He said if it were not for Mom, he would not have the life he now had. He said Mom gave him his beautiful life. Stories like this make it clear that Mom's life mattered more than she knew.

I want to send her on vacations she has never taken and send her places she only read about in books. I want her to know I am her child and she is my mother, but all I can do is wish and hope for these two things, because none of what I wish or hope for Mom will ever come to pass.

ON BEING STUBBORN

I took Mom for a walk yesterday. It was the beginning of summer 2014 and she needed to be out of the house.

Currently she is walking at a much slower pace than she used to. She complains that her "stupid foot" is hurting. For the first time in years, she has told me her legs and hip are also aching. Since Mom became ill, she seldom gets sick. I cannot recall the last time she had a cold. Forget about the flu; that is nonexistent in her world. She never gets a fever. How can this be? I am not sure if it's the medication, but whatever it is, it is a mystery. We all get sick sometimes, but that does not apply to her.

At times she will tell me she is old, and at other times she tells me she is young. Today she seems much older than she is because she is walking like a little old lady.

Mom is very old for her seventy-four years. This is one of the things this disease does to its victims; it ages them beyond their actual earthly years. She was always so beautiful, with flawless skin. It seems like only a few weeks ago she was very active, but now she shuffles along.

While on our walk, she spotted a penny on the street. She said she saw something while pointing to the ground, and then she stopped and started to bend over. I told her she should not be picking things up in the street and gently tugged on her hand. "I see something on the ground and I am going to pick it up," she insisted. I kept pulling on her hand while she continued to resist. I finally had to give in, and she retrieved the penny.

Each day I beg the Lord to allow me to outlive her. If she outlives me, that will be really horrible for her! No one else

185

wants her around. It's too much work, and she is too stubborn and never listens. My prayers are not for selfish reasons but for her sake. I need to see this through with her to the end. In my opinion, it would be the biggest tragedy if I had to leave her behind in this world.

IN THE EYES OF THE BEHOLDER

The first weekend in summer 2014 was beautiful. The sun was out all day both Saturday and Sunday. I picked Mom up as usual and headed to church.

I was a speaker in the first portion of the service. I usually officiated on the first Saturday of the month. My topic was kindness. The focus of the fifteen-minute talk was: "How would your behavior change if you found out you would die at midnight?" The premise was that people would probably be nice for the last day of their life, and if they could be nice for the last day, they should act this way on a daily basis. I also said we were usually kind to strangers and not so kind to the people closest to us. I told the audience we should change how we act and be kind to our loved ones. I challenged them to be kind no matter what was going on in their lives.

After church we went back to my house for lunch. Then Stephen and I took Mom to Home Depot to keep her occupied. He picked up a few items while Mom pushed the cart, and for a brief moment she seemed to be with us both in body and mind. She was chatting and made a bit of sense. For a few fleeting moments, the world was a blissful place, the wind blowing through the trees, the birds chirping in the background—at least, that was what I was thinking. The trip to the store was one of the best we'd had with her in a long time.

We took Mom home at around 6:30. It was a very long day for her. When we arrived, Ms. Muffin and several members of our family were sitting on the patio having an early dinner. A family friend was visiting the United States and prior to our arrival he had been the only male in the group. He usually wore a baseball cap and dark sunglasses when he was outside.

I left Mom on the patio and went inside. Upon my return, I was unsure what the topic of conservation was. Mom was now seated close to the table on the patio with the rest of the family.

As the conversation progressed, our friend got up to illustrate something he was talking about. He had a small stick in his hand and was waving his hands as he related his story. Mom kept a close eye on him. As he gestured he bent down, and as he did Mom said in a loud voice that he looked like a monkey.

Everyone began to laugh uncontrollably at her comment. What else could we do but laugh?

THE LORD IS MY SHEPHERD

Sally's new home has a three-season porch. It's great when they have a BBQ; anyone sitting in it is shielded from the sun, dust, and all the winged creatures of summer. I love the porch because I am not a fan of most of the creatures that fly around in the summertime. I hate flies and gnats.

Sally had a cookout a few weeks ago. They had chairs and two tables on the porch, and she had at least fifteen of us sitting there. Just before lunch was served, I asked Mom to say the grace before the meal. She slowly rose from her chair and announced that everyone should stand up. Sally and Tara remained seated, and Mom snapped at them, "Stand up!" Once we all were standing, she said, "Bow your heads."

I stood next to her, holding her hand. The day before she had seemed particularly fragile and it had not improved. I thought perhaps I should stand close to her to give her some support.

She began by saying Psalm 23, "The Lord is my Shepherd." She said the entire psalm without missing a word. I was so surprised.

She had forgotten so many things, yet she could remember the psalm so well. In addition to the psalm, she prayed for people who are less fortunate and then prayed for the food. Midway through her prayers, I began to cry. Why? I cried for her because of the way her life had turned out. I cried for myself because I could not comprehend what had gone wrong with her, and I basically cried for all of us who were gathered there because none of us knows exactly what will happen to us in the future. Even in Mom's darkness, somehow she had managed to pull out of that beaten-up brain something with no error.

May God have mercy on her, because He is the only one who may be able to come to her rescue. When she dies, I hope she will finally have peace.

THE DOCTOR

Mom had a doctor's appointment. We normally see Dr. Matthew on a monthly basis. If Mom is behaving well, he will tell me to come back in two months; if her behavior changes, he will see her immediately. I jokingly refer to him as her drug dealer. Each time we see him, it's less than fifteen minutes. We never leave empty-handed. Quite honestly, I hate visiting him, but if we do not do so, she will have no medication and without the medication she becomes totally mad. All of the symptoms that are suppressed appear and everything spins out of control; we can't do anything with her.

On the way to the doctor, Mom kept telling me she had to stop by my house because she had to drop off some money for Stephen. She was convinced she owed him money, and it made her sad. According to her, she hid the money in a can. Once he got home she wanted to hug and kiss him and give him his money.

She then changed the subject; she wanted me to know that she had stolen something. When I asked what she had stolen, she admitted it was a fig. She said a little boy brought it to her. When I questioned why she had stolen the fig, she said she could not steal because God would turn His back on her if she did. I reassured her God would never do something like that, but of course by this time she had changed the subject once again.

We arrived at the doctor's office. As soon as we got there, she began telling me she had to leave. I pointed to the receptionist area and told her the ladies had told us to sit and wait. She got up and began walking, so I moved close to the exit to stop her from leaving. She got so angry at me and was about to go into one of her rages, but thankfully the doctor came and called her name then. As we were walking down the hall, she told him he was handsome.

We sat down and he asked her how she was. She tried to answer but failed. She went on to another subject. She told him again that he was handsome, but she added that he needed to lose a little weight. When we were young, Mom used to say, "Any girl should have three things in life—she should be pretty, skinny, and have some money." Even now that she is ill, if she saw someone who was overweight, she would still say, "Oh my, [he or she] is so fat."

The doctor asked me how Mom was doing. I told him, he sent in her prescription, and the entire visit including our wait time took less than fifteen minutes.

This is the life we now live with Ms. B.

THE BBQ

It was July 4, 2014. We were having a BBQ at my house. I invited the family over for a late lunch. We started to eat around 4:30. I had assumed that after dinner, when it became dark, everyone would want to go and enjoy the fireworks. The town I live in has a beautiful display each year. I asked if anyone wanted to go, but everyone declined.

As the afternoon grew into evening, I put citronella oil into two beautiful containers that I normally light to keep the bugs away. We were all sitting on the patio when I lit them. As usual, I kept a close eye on Mom's every move.

She wore a beautiful long summer dress that day. It had actually rained most of the day, but the sun finally made an appearance at around 4:00. As it got progressively darker, the wind picked up. It had turned out to be a wonderful day, and the evening was really lovely.

Mom got out of the chair and slowly walked over to the first lit container. I got up and walked behind her. She was about to bend over the container when I stood in her way. She became annoyed and said, "I simply wanted to see if the fire was hot." She moved around me, then bent down and put her hand close to the flame. I grabbed her hand and she yanked it away from me. "Do you think I am stupid enough to touch it?" As she spoke, she again tried to touch the container.

The wind blew her flowing dress closer and closer to the flames. I got scared and called Stephen to get Mom. On his way over, Mom picked up her dress and walked over to the second flame, and was about to drop her dress over the flame when Stephen called her. She turned and let go of her dress, and it came billowing down so close to the flame that I had to kick the container away. She had no idea that her being so close to the flame was dangerous. Once Stephen got her attention, I extinguished the flames and told everyone we had to go inside. The concept of danger was all but lost to her.

192

CRAP

Mom's previous life was always so busy in contrast to what it is now, just a crawl. No one would have imagined this for her.

Mom and I are still going to church each week. We still stay for lunch. On this particular day, we were sitting at lunch when she announced out loud, "I have to shit." I accompanied her to the bathroom, and as I walked in behind her she said, "Leave the room." I told her I would be just outside the door and, with that said I closed the door behind me to give her some privacy.

I attend a small church where there is one bathroom for the ladies and one for the men. On this day we had several visitors, and people kept coming to use the bathroom. I had to turn them away. After waiting for about ten minutes, I knocked on the door and said I was coming in. I walked in and found Mom sitting halfway off the toilet bowl with a piece of toilet paper in her hand that she had used to clean herself.

"B, throw the dirty toilet paper in the toilet," I said.

"I need to wet it to clean myself properly," she responded. The more I insisted she put the toilet paper in the bowl, the more she insisted she needed it wet.

I walked over to her and stretched my hand out in anticipation of her giving the toilet paper to me. She refused to hand it over. I took her hand and tried to retrieve it.

She immediately tightened her fist around it. I attempted to pry her fingers open as I struggled to get the paper. I kept asking her to give the paper to me, but she refused. She was still seated on the toilet as I physically forced open one finger at a time in order to retrieve the dirty toilet paper. I was totally disgusted with her. In addition, I was disgusted with the entire situation. When I had left home that morning, it never occurred to me that a few hours later I would be locked in a bathroom fighting Mom to get a piece of toilet paper full of shit.

As we continued to struggle for the toilet paper, I noticed her hand had shit on it; to make the situation worse, so did mine. When I finally got the mangled toilet paper out of her hands, I asked her to move off the toilet so I could throw the paper in the bowl, but she refused to move. I had no choice but to dump the dirty toilet paper in the garbage. I washed my hands several times, then got several clean pieces of toilet paper and handed them to her one piece at a time. Still sitting on the toilet seat, she tried her best to clean herself off and kept requesting that I wet the paper. At this point the damage was done, and I handed her a dry piece, then a wet piece, of toilet paper. She cleaned herself off and I finally got her off the toilet seat. I quickly flushed the toilet and washed her hands.

When she was finished I tried opening the bathroom door. She said, "Wait." Then she adjusted her dress, took both hands, and brushed her hair back.

We finally walked out of the bathroom after twenty minutes. I felt horrible for having arm wrestled Mom for her shit. As we walked away, I knew she had already forgotten what had happened, but I had not. I was now feeling sick. I thought I was going to vomit.

We returned to the lunchroom, and I allowed her to finish lunch. When we left, I was too upset to speak to anyone. Once we got on the road, she began talking about the cars and the houses and how smart I was to find my way around. That day I was not feeling smart at all. As a matter of fact, I felt like crap!

CAR INCIDENT

We received an invitation to visit a friend of mine living in upstate New York. I decided to take Mom along for the long ride. It would give her the opportunity to see all the things she claimed she had never seen before. She had a great time on the car ride there.

When we arrived I introduced Mom to the family. Mom was enthralled by the children and kept telling them how beautiful they were, while sharing hugs and kisses repeatedly.

It was a lovely day. We had lunch on the deck. After lunch, Mom asked to sit on the front porch in the sun. On the way to the porch, she stumbled and almost fell. There was nothing on the floor. I assumed she must have taken a misstep because she was shuffling her feet and stumbled.

I followed Mom out the door and moved a rocker into the sun where she could sit. She sat down and looked straight ahead, and she rocked for the remainder of the visit.

Once we were ready to leave, I took Mom to the bathroom. We said our good-byes. Several of us were visiting my friend that day, so we had taken two cars on the trip. Stephen was the lead driver and I followed him. The house we visited was off the main road and nestled on a hill. The private driveway had several twists and turns.

As I began making my way down the driveway, Mom saw the kids and my friend waving good-bye. She opened the back door in an effort to exit the vehicle. Luckily, she was buckled in. I could clearly see my friend gasp as the back door swung open.

Ms. Muffin was sitting next to Mom, and she quickly instructed her to close the door. Thankfully, Mom listened. As I drove past my friend, I lowered the front window and told her this behavior was "par for the course."

THIS DISEASE

Mom is significantly worse now than she was a couple of years ago. As the disease progresses, it changes; her violent outbursts, thank the Lord, are gone, but so is she.

Like most family members who have someone with this disease, I read every article I can find about Alzheimer's. I read not just for information but to see if somewhere in the near future there might be hope for some unknown family who, like me, is watching and desperately praying that there will be some kind of breakthrough.

I know it's too late for Mom. I have prepared myself for what is coming in the near future. However, I must confess it's very difficult to watch her slip away. I know her decline is part of the disease, but to watch it on a daily basis and not be able to do one little thing to slow it down is heartbreaking. It's been years since we first confirmed she was ill. She is now a totally different person. She will tell us she saw someone or had a conversation with someone, but the people she is supposedly speaking with died decades ago. What part of the brain can fool her so badly that she is incapable of remembering that the dead do not speak?

We sit together and she will tell me she just saw someone go up or down the stairs when the two of us are the only ones in the house. She will tell me she just left the children in the house when the children, whoever they are, were never there in the first place. She is always telling me that my niece was just with us and now she cannot find her. I often wonder what is going on in her mind that causes her to see these phantoms.

EVER-PRESENT FEAR

As a child, I had two persistent fears: First, I was afraid of water, and because I could not swim I was afraid if I ventured into the water, I would drown. The second was being caught in a fire and not being able to escape the flames. When I became an adult, I learned to swim, thereby eliminating one of my fears. The second one—well, let's just say I have not found the equivalent of swimming in fire yet, so this one still lingers.

After Mom became ill I developed a third fear: a constant and nagging fear of becoming like her and losing my mind. Becoming like Mom is the worst type of fear. For the past few years, I have had an up-close and personal view of what it's like to lose one's mind. This has been the worst experience I've had thus far in my life.

Each day I live, the fear is there and intensifying. If I forget to close the closet door, if I forget someone's name, if I see a spot in my eyeball—no matter what it is—I freak out. My head is always buzzing with what I should do if I think I am getting this disease. At times the fear makes me think that I will go insane. No matter how I try to shake the fear, it does not go away. It is a constant and annoying companion. I liken it to falling off a hill into a pile of shit, and the only thing you can do is smell the shit as it gets closer and closer and you know there is nothing you can do about it.

AN UNWALLED CITY

I recently read an article that described all humans as cursed with death, and it used the analogy of death as "living in an unwalled city."

To the ancients, a city without walls was worse than living on the plains, as it offered no protection from plundering enemies. At least if you were on the plains you would be vigilant, but in a city with no walls, one could become complacent. Living in a walled city offered protection because those walls kept the enemies out, and even if the enemies tried to get in, they could be seen in advance so preparations could be made to foil an attack.

I was thinking the other day that our skull is the wall that protects the brain from harm. But this wall offers no protection from Alzheimer's. It's akin to building Babylon-like walls, so wide that chariots rode on them. But this disease simply seems to glide over, or get under, the skull wall unnoticed, quietly becoming the unwanted guest, while everyone is watching outside, guarding against threats. It slowly but surely steals and destroys everything in the brain. By the time one notices, it is too late. This disease takes everything and destroys its host as an unwalled city not offering any protection from the enemy.

A CHANGE IN THE AIR

It was February 2015. A week ago, Ms. Muffin called me very early in the morning. She wanted me to know Mom's breast was bleeding. Mom had breast cancer several years ago, and this was exactly how it had begun. I suspected the cancer had returned.

The first time around I had been a bit anxious about the diagnosis, but this time I was very calm. I made an appointment with the cancer specialist. The appointment was made for a few days later. When the day came, I picked Mom up from day care and drove her to the doctor's office. When we arrived we did not have to wait. We were shown to the examining room immediately, where the nurse told Mom to undress. The nurse left us, promising to return with the doctor.

Mom refused to take her clothes off. We had such a fight. When I told her to take her sweater off, she said she was cold and was not going to take the sweater off. I told her the doctor needed to see her chest and she had to take her sweater off. I tried to take the sweater off for her, but she pushed me away. Eventually she began to take the sweater off. She struggled to do it, but finally it came off. Under the sweater she had on an undershirt; it was a bit tight and I knew she would not be able to get it off herself, so I moved closer to assist her. She put her hand up and said, "I will do it myself. Leave me alone." She began taking off the undershirt, but somehow it got stuck on her face. I went over to assist her and finally got the undershirt off, then came the bra. I unclipped the back of the bra, and she quickly held the strap close to her body thinking I could not get the bra off. I had to pry her fingers off one at a time to take the bra off.

S. P. Murray

I put the gown on her. Immediately she tried to take the gown off. I did my best to distract her. There were some magazines in the room; I asked if she wanted to look at a few of them. "No," she replied. I walked over to the rack and took a few of the magazines, and quickly found some brightly colored dresses to show her. Once that got her attention, she came over and I began turning the pages slowly while talking to her about the clothes.

We were in the room for approximately ten minutes before the doctor and the nurse arrived. I was relieved to see them. By the time they arrived, my head was aching and my stomach was in a knot. The doctor introduced himself and began speaking to Mom. She didn't follow the conversation well and was unable to answer any of his questions.

He told Mom he was going to examine her and that she should lie down on the bed. The nurse pulled out a section of the bed for Mom to rest her feet, but she did not want to lie down. I walked over and stroked her back, telling her the doctor had to do an examination of her breast and she had to lie back so he could see it. Finally, after several minutes, she complied.

He conducted his examination and squeezed her nipple; when he did, a dark fluid excreted. He put the liquid in a bottle for testing. He wanted Mom to have a scan, but after seeing her in her noncompliant state, he knew she would not be able to lie in the machine for forty-five minutes. The scan was out of the question.

After the examination, the doctor sat down and spoke with Mom for another thirty minutes. I suppose he was attempting to gauge her mental state. He asked her about her children. She gave him some answer that had nothing to do with his question, but he continued speaking. He complimented me, saying I had a nice mom and it seemed we took very good care of her.

Before the doctor left, he said something that made a lot of sense. He said if the cancer had recurred she could live approximately seven years. In Mom's current state of mind, he assumed with her disease she could live another seven years. Therefore, if she had cancer, why bother to torture her, given

200

that with both diseases her life span was approximately seven years?

I could have kissed him (I did not); not many doctors are this honest. The majority of them seem to push all kinds of treatment no matter how sick the patient is. I thanked him for his honesty. He left us in the room and I got Mom dressed without incident.

The nurse stayed in the room and chatted with Mom. She told the nurse how beautiful she was and kissed her a few times. We walked back to the nurses' station; the doctor was not too far away, and when I walked over and said good-bye to him, Mom took his hands and kissed him. She said to him, "It was very nice to meet you, Dr. Breast." We all had a good laugh about the new name he had received.

The test results would be available in a week. Once again, we began the waiting game. Were the test results going to be negative or positive for cancer? If the cancer had returned, then what? In her current state, if she tested positive for cancer and they operated, she would have to be physically restrained, possibly, until she healed. The first time she had cancer, it was in the early stages. When she had that operation, she told me she wanted no further treatment. I honored her wishes then.

I drove Mom home. On the drive, I was trying to decide what I was going to do, while replaying in my head what the doctor had said. I decided the doctor had a valid point. If she would live for seven years either way, why do surgery that would add only pain and frustration to her life and nothing else?

I am the one who has to make all her medical decisions. No matter what I do, I never seem to win one little fight for her, and I suspected this time would not be different. I have convinced myself that I am playing God with her life, managing her care the way I see fit because she is incapable of managing it herself. Playing God with her life is difficult.

A few months ago, I had to give a talk in church and chose the subject of pagan gods. I did some research and found an article with the heading "Where Have All the Gods Gone?" Let me assure you that many pagan gods may have disappeared, but while I am not a pagan, I have been added to the list of the "gods."

A few days after we visited the doctor, I made the decision: When I got the phone call from the doctor's office, no matter what the result was, I decided she would not have surgery. The doctor's office never called and I never followed up with them. What was the point? I had made the decision for her to live with whatever was going on in her breast. Once again we were living with the unknown, so we wait for whatever the future holds for her, and for me.

LOOKING BACK TO 2010

Mom's disease really took a firm hold of her in 2010, even though there were signs prior to that. I can say it really reared its ugly head prominently at that time.

It is now 2015, and with each passing month more and more things keep kept going wrong with her. Most of the time Mom has no idea who I am. It is something that is very difficult for me to deal with, but then again, what choice do I have but to play along with whomever she wishes me to be?

I have no children of my own. However, I am now called upon to be a parent to her. How do you learn to deal with an adult who is really a child, especially when you have no formal training for the role? I hope I can fulfill this role for her with as few mistakes as possible.

I often look into her eyes to try and see the Mom I once knew, but the "who" and "what" she used to be are now gone. Once in a while she will ask me why I look at her the way I do. I give her some silly response, knowing it really does not matter because in less than thirty seconds she will forget she asked me the question.

I try my best to be there for her as much as possible. I hang on to her as a mother would her child. She does not always appreciate the handholding, because sometimes she will wiggle her hands out of mine and tell me to go ahead. I sometimes reluctantly comply and will always call to her to be sure she is right behind me. Sometimes she answers, but at other times she simply gets impatient with me and says something mean under her breath. I guess that is what some children do to their parents. I really don't care what she says. I need to keep her safe.

Caring for Mom is beyond stressful. I have to think about each and every thing, no matter how small it is. A friend of mine reminded me the other day that many caregivers die, leaving the sick person behind. She warned me never to let this happen to me. My days are consumed with thoughts of what I can do to make her life better, but no matter what I do it is never enough.

She is living in her own world. Her reality is not my reality because she no longer sees the things I see. I know one day soon she will cease to recognize whoever she thinks I am. When that day comes, I hope I will be able to bear that burden. I am sad now, but when she does not remember me any longer, that will be even sadder. Can you imagine your mom not knowing who you are?

This is one of the hardest things anyone can go through. I often wonder if Mom actually knows what is occurring in her daily life. I know she does not, although deep down I hope that she does. I also hope, for her sake, that she is happy and somehow she understands that she is loved, if not by many then at least a few. I still want the best for her and will do almost anything to give that to her. I still hope that she realizes how hard Stephen and I try to give her a good home and a comfortable life. Even if she does not, we know in our hearts that we are doing our best for her. Hopefully, as long as she lives we can keep doing all we can to give her a good life.

IN GOD'S WAITING ROOM

I was speaking to a friend of mine several months ago and told her if I really wanted to be morbid about life, I could say that humans never actually live. From the day we are conceived, we begin the personal trek that ends in death; no matter who we are, no matter what we accomplish, we all end up dead sooner or later!

Ms. Muffin told me the other day, "We are all walking on our roof." I did not understand the statement, so I asked her to explain what she meant. She said, "Our final resting place is six feet under. Therefore, the earth is our roof." I thought that was a great observation!

I was watching this television show recently called *From the Cradle to the Grave*, and it showed the journey from birth to death. When you really look at it, humans have a very short life span. We are truly nothing. The show made me remember what a friend had told me not long ago. He said, "When we retire and move to Florida, we move into God's waiting room." Life is like a waiting room. Even better, it's like a doctor's waiting room; there we are simply waiting for our name to be called when our appointed time comes.

There is death, there is dying, there is dying with dignity, and then there's Alzheimer's—a death while you are still alive, but in reality you are dead. How can one be alive but dead, you may ask? You can when you have this disease.

Alzheimer's calls, "You are next!" But it does not kill you. Well, it does not kill your body, but it kills the mind. So, it's almost like your "next," but not really, because with Alzheimer's your heart is beating but your brain is dead.

The brain is gone, but the heart keeps pumping. The disease extracts everything from its victims, leaving a tiny shell behind.

It leaves people unaware they are waiting for the final call of "next."

These days I have been thinking about so many different scenarios for Mom's "next." I have a colleague who is an expert on many topics. We had a conversation a few weeks ago and, just to tease him and get one of his educated responses, I told him animals are smarter than people. As expected, he went into a tizzy and disagreed completely.

I told him if he believed in God (and I know he does), the Bible specifically states that animals were called into existence before man. I continued by saying that, in my opinion, you make the more important things first rather than last. Furthermore, when man was made, God instructed him to take care of the animals. In our daily routine, if we own animals, they do not clean up after us; to the contrary, they create the mess and we do all the cleaning. Hence, I must be correct that they are more important.

My colleague was beside himself trying to prove me wrong. He wanted to know how on God's green earth I could say something like that. He said animals have no understanding of things and they do not think the way we do. (I don't believe this at all). I listened, then gave him another point to consider. I said in great disasters, when they are not tethered or otherwise restrained, animals head for higher ground or simply leave the epicenter of the upcoming disaster. In my opinion, we hold our animals in higher esteem than we do our fellow citizens.

My friend did not have a suitable comeback for my argument. He was not convinced, but I had a bigger point yet to make. I said that most everyone loves and cares for their pets and would not want any harm to befall them. When they are in pain, weak, and frail, we mercifully put them to sleep to avoid the constant agony of living. But in our "civil" society, as we call it, we have no exit plans for ourselves or our fellow humans. We strenuously avoid using the word "death" in the United States. We say people have passed away or that we are putting our pets to sleep. Death seems to be a taboo topic. Why? I do not know.

So to you reading these words of my journey on these humble pages, I pose the question: How is it we are so kind to our pets when they are terminally ill, but we cannot extend that same compassion to our friends and family?

Mom wanders through life as a shadow of what she once was. Her "next" in God's waiting room is long gone, and only a tiny portion of who she was is waiting for the appointed call—a call that, when it comes, she will be unable to comprehend. That understanding for her was lost a long time ago. How or why was her "next" taken away so cruelly?

THE WALK

In early Spring 2015, it was a lot easier to take Mom for walks. At that time she seemed to really love going out for walks. These days, she does not seem at all interested anymore.

I visited her yesterday and she was in such a lighthearted mood. This made me so happy. After dinner she agreed to go for a walk with me. She can no longer walk very fast, so it's more like a stroll. We walked down the street and crossed over at the end of the block, then walked two blocks down. One of the train lines in her town is only for freight trains, and as we were walking we saw the freight train go by with all the loaded containers. We stood for several minutes as the train went by. I counted over one hundred cars. Once it passed and the gates were lifted, we crossed over the tracks and walked past a small creek that ran close by.

There is a bridge over the creek, and as we walked on it we paused and I told Mom to look down to see if there were any fish. The water, though flowing, was quite clear, allowing us to see the rocks at the shallow bottom of the creek. There were lilies in the water, and some of them were blooming.

At the side of the creek, there was a plethora of rocks, which she did not recognize. She said they were some sort of small animal.

I kept pressing her, asking if she saw any fish, but she kept saying she did not. I didn't see any myself. We moved on and turned the corner, then proceeded up a small incline where we lost sight of the bridge and creek. Midway up the little hill, Mom announced she had to go to the bathroom. We turned down the first street we saw to head back home. The creek flowed past this street; there was a small hill and we descended it, passing the creek a second time. I noticed the grass and little shrubs around the waterway, which came very close to the street. The shrubs were tall, stately, and quite picturesque.

Mom asked me what type of bush the shrub was. I said they were pussy willows. "Pussy willows!" she exclaimed in a loud voice. "I don't see any pussies in those bushes." It made me laugh. It was then I realized I had used the wrong name for the shrubs. I told her that I had made a mistake and the plants were called cattails. She simply looked at me in disbelief and kept saying, "No tails, no cats."

Five minutes later, we finished our walk and arrived home. By this time, she had completely forgotten about the bathroom. When I asked her if she needed to go to the bathroom, she said no. She sat down on the chair and began to watch TV.

WHISKEY LULLABY

As the years roll along, I've become more obsessive when it comes to reading material on this disease. I guess I am hoping that one day I will find something that offers some kind of assurance and gives me hope that there will be a light at the end of the tunnel—instead of the train that is now rolling down the track at one hundred miles an hour and will hit whatever it finds in its way.

Mom always loved to sing. I read that music is good for someone in her condition, so whenever I am around her I play music for her.

I have always loved the music from the 1970s and 1980s, including country music. When we are driving and the music is on, she will hum along, and at other times, when the stars are truly aligned, she might be able to sing a few words in a song. I smile from ear to ear in those rare fleeting moments. Lately, I play a lot of country music; it mirrors my mood because most country music deals with some kind of loss, and God knows we have lost a lot.

On one of our driving excursions a couple of months ago, Mom and I were listening to a song, named "Whiskey Lullaby." As with many country ballads, it was about a woman who left a man, and he was so brokenhearted he drank himself to death. And she, even though she had left him, never quite got over her love for him and drank herself to death too. Mom sat quietly, and before the end of the song, she asked, "They killed themselves?"

"That is correct," I told her.

She said, "That is sad." I agreed with her.

At times she can understand some things so perfectly. And then, just like that, the ability vanishes. These days, when she has these moments, it is so startling for me—just like that, *PING*, she lights up my world, and just as quickly as it comes, it goes away and once again the darkness of her disease falls on me like a ton of bricks.

THE SPELL, WHATEVER IT WAS

It is now July 2015, and for the past three weeks Mom has been in such a good mood. I wish she could stay this way forever. When she is like this, it reminds me of when she was well.

Sally and her family are on vacation, and since their departure Mom has not been angry once. I assume her exceptionally good mood has to do with their not being around. Do I know this for a fact? No, but what other explanation could there be?

On Saturday, July 25, Mom and I went to church. She looked so pretty. She was wearing an off-white dress with tiny pink flowers on the bodice, and each flower was surrounded with white crystal beads.

After lunch we returned to my house. Mom sat at the table in the dining room, turning the pages of a book as though she was reading. She sat there for about ten minutes. Shortly thereafter, she went upstairs to use the bathroom. I followed her up and we came back down together.

It was a beautiful day. I asked her if she wanted to sit outside and she agreed. We both went out on the back steps and sat down on the top step. I told her I would put a towel down on the step so her pretty dress would not get dirty. I went back into the kitchen, found a towel, put it down, and she and I sat down. She took her shoes off and I noticed her toenails were a bit long. I said I was going to cut her toenails and she said okay. Small victory! I feel compelled to mention this because she is always so uncooperative, yet she had just agreed to do something without being nagged.

I went back into the house and got the nail clipper and a nail file. I returned in less than two minutes and began cutting her toenails. When I was finished, I noticed she had a callus under her big toe. I told her I was going to file it down, and again she said okay. Another victory! I thought, *This is a great day for me; twice in a row she said yes.* I wasted no time at all and began to file the callus down.

A couple of minutes later, she said, "I am dizzy." I was surprised, because usually she is unable to tell us how she feels. I repeated what she said, and again she said, "I am dizzy." Less than a minute later, both of her hands began shaking uncontrollably.

I got up quickly and got in front of her. "What is the matter?" She said nothing. She began to sweat and her complexion turned chalk white. My niece was visiting me that day and I called her and asked her to bring some tissues to wipe Mom's face. Once I got the tissues, I asked again what was wrong. Mom tried to answer me. However, when she tried to speak her speech was garbled—nothing except some funny sounds came out of her mouth. I was still standing in front of her, and by this time my niece was sitting behind her bracing her up. Mom tried to move her hand toward her leg, but her hand was shaking so badly it just kept hitting her. She then tried to hold on to the railing on the step. I guess she was trying to get up, but she could not hold on to anything. I told her not to move.

I asked my niece to get the phone and some water for me, and she quickly returned with both items. I gave Mom a little water to drink. She then moved her head forward, and I thought she was about to pass out. When her head came forward, a small amount of the water came out of her mouth, along with a long line of spit. By this time she was making heaving sounds, almost like she could not breathe. She was cold to the touch. I really thought she was dying.

My niece again sat behind Mom and I called 911. In a few minutes the police, fire department, and an ambulance were at the house. Everyone was trying to ask Mom questions. Of course, she could not respond. I explained that she has Alzheimer's and would not be able to answer any questions. I answered all the questions they asked. She was put on a stretcher and wheeled to the waiting ambulance. The attendant wanted to know if I would drive with them to the hospital. I told them I wanted to drive my car; the hospital is less than one mile from my home.

I arrived at the emergency room before they did and waited outside. Once they got there she was wheeled into the hospital and down the hall to a room. I gave the nurse Mom's insurance information and her records were accessed.

A few minutes passed before a young technician came in, introduced himself, and told me Mom was scheduled for a CT scan. I explained that Mom might not be able to have the scan because she would try to get out of the bed. He informed me that they strapped patients like her to the bed and said she should be fine. I was allowed to accompany her to the room.

Mom was wheeled down two long corridors, finally coming to the room where the test was going to be performed. There were two other people in the room, and they began to explain to Mom what they were going to do. I had to repeat my story that she has Alzheimer's and did not understand what they were telling her. The explanation continued and I stood outside the door. She was told about the machine, how they were going to move her from the bed to the machine, the board they were going to place under her in order to get her from one bed to the other. I just stood there and looked on. Finally, they got her into the machine. Someone said to her, "Don't worry, this will not hurt. Think of this as taking a picture, but it is just a picture of your head." They wrapped her up tightly, put a strap over her head, and told her, "Now lie still and this will only take two minutes." They came out the door in a rush, closed the door behind them, and went into another room to begin their work.

All the rooms along this hallway had huge glass windows; she was in one room, they were in the room next to her, and I was in the hallway watching them watch her. I could see her lying there.

One of the young men sat down at his computer and began his work. Less than fifteen seconds after he sat down, I saw Mom's head pop up. "How did that happen?" someone asked. The technician got out of his chair, ran back into the room, and secured Mom's head again. As he was closing the door, I told him he had to tell her to be still. He took my advice and started telling Mom that he would be finished soon and to stay still. I guess Mom wanted him to know she had heard him, so all of a sudden I saw her hand go up and give a little wave. If I were not so scared, I would have had a good laugh, but this was not funny. I was not sure what was going on with her and was afraid that perhaps she'd had a stroke or something worse.

Again the young man popped out of his seat, ran back into the room, and secured her hand. He came back into the room, but this time he did not call her by her name. He just told her to be still and assured her he would be finished in a minute. He repeated this a couple of times, and this time he got the job done.

Once he was finished, the instructions started all over again; they told her how they were going to roll her back into the bed. Once this was done, they covered her up, wheeled her out, and down the hallway we went, back to the room.

Approximately ten minutes later, the nurse came and began opening up vials. I informed her she could not do anything intravenously. Whatever she had to give Mom had to be oral because she would rip off anything that was put on her. The nurse said she would have to check with the doctor. In the ambulance they had attached some tags to her body because they were monitoring her on the short ride to the hospital. She had already removed the little tag that had been on her leg and was working on the one close to her shoulder.

Mom was told to hold her hand out. When she did, the nurse placed a small device on her finger. It looked like an old-fashioned clothespin. Once attached, the monitor above Mom's head came to life and began monitoring her vital signs. The nurse left, and a few minutes later someone else came in to test her blood sugar. Again I had to explain that Mom has Alzheimer's and would not understand any of the instructions given. The technician just went ahead and explained to Mom that she would feel a pinch when he pricked her finger. When he pricked her finger, she tried to pull her hand away, but she was not successful in her attempt. The sample was taken and off he went.

In the five and a half hours Mom was in the hospital, they ran approximately six tests and wanted to run more. Not long after the nurse and technician left, Mom raised her hand and declared, "This is hurting my finger." She took the little clip off and laid it on the bed; no matter how many times I put it back on her finger, she just kept taking it off. She did not understand this was something she needed to keep on her finger. Along with the clip on her finger, the nurse had attached a blood pressure cuff on her arm. Mom said it was squeezing her, so she just peeled it off and threw it off the bed. She was a bit tangled in the wires, so in order to free herself she just began pulling them off. By now the overhead machine was making all kinds of noise and I could see a flat green line going across the machine.

Once she got all the wires off, she began to come off the bed, even though the nurse had the two handlebars up on both sides of the bed. Mom slid down, came off the bed, and headed for the door.

"B, we are in the hospital. You cannot leave," I said. She ignored me and left the room. I spotted the nurse down the hall, ran toward her, and asked her for assistance in getting Mom back into the room. The nurse came over and, in a sweet voice, told Mom she had to get back into the bed. Mom listened to her and followed her back into the room. The bed was lowered and Mom got back on. I told the nurse she would not stay in the bed because she got restless in the evening and it was now past 6:00. The nurse then lowered the front of the bed. Mom's feet were now much higher than her head, so there was no way she could get up.

A few minutes later the nurse came back and informed me she had been told by the doctor that Mom had to have the IV. By now I was more than annoyed; I had explained and explained Mom's condition to so many technicians and nurses that I was getting quite sick of it. No one looked at the computer to see her chart. They all just came in and tried to do what they needed to do, and here I was explaining the same thing over and over again. When the nurse declared her intentions as per the doctor's instructions, I guess my annoyance showed because I raised my voice and told her that no IV was going in Mom's arm. I explained, yet again, that Mom would rip the needle out and there would be blood all over the place. I pointed to the blood pressure cuff and clip that were both lying on the floor and told her that this was where the line and needle would end up.

The nurse got a bit upset and walked to the door; in a loud voice, she called out, "Doctor, the daughter is refusing treatment for her mom." I began saying that I was not refusing treatment but, before I could finish, out the door she went. I never had the chance to finish what I was saying. A few minutes later the doctor came, and once again I had to explain to her my rationale for not wanting the IV. The doctor seemed to understand and said perhaps they would have to keep her overnight to be monitored. I said I would not agree for her to be admitted because I did not want her tied to the bed all night long. The doctor understood my request and said that hopefully the tests results would be in shortly and they would be able to determine what had happened. She left and we never saw her again.

The X-ray technician came in and I helped her take Mom's dress off. Once she was undressed I was asked to leave the room. When the X-rays were done, the technician for the blood came and drew blood while I tried to keep Mom as calm as possible. Then, finally, the man with the pee cup came and told me they needed a sample. I explained to him there was no way Mom would be able to pee in the cup, and once more I had to explain to him why. He said she would have to try. We had now been in the hospital for over four hours; the shift had changed and new nurses and doctors had come on duty. Mom kept trying to get out of the bed but could not do so.

Finally, a new nurse came in and said, "Oh! I see you did not do the urine sample."

I explained the same thing to her that I had now explained to six other workers in the hospital: Mom has Alzheimer's and she was unable to do certain things.

"She is incontinent?" asked the nurse.

I said, "No, she is not incontinent, but she is unable to give the pee sample."

"Then we will have to put a catheter in."

In the sternest voice I could muster, I said, "No such thing will be done. There will be no urine sample given."

She left the room. I waited for another ten minutes, and when no one returned I finally went to the nurses' station and asked how long the test results would be. "We are waiting on the urine sample" was the answer. I again stated, this time in a much harsher voice, "There will no urine sample. I've said this to several nurses and one technician. She is unable to do the urine test! Give me the results of the other tests that you took and we will leave." The nurse looked in the computer and confirmed all the results were in, but we would have to speak to the new doctor who had just begun his shift. He should be in to see us shortly.

I walked back to the room, and Mom asked to go to the bathroom. Somehow I was able to adjust the bed to a normal level. I helped her out of bed, put her clothes on, and we walked down the hall to the bathroom.

We went into the bathroom and Mom walked over to the toilet. I was about to get a piece of paper towel to wipe the seat when I turned and saw she was in the process of sitting down. I told her to wait, but she ignored me and sat down on the wet toilet seat. I rolled out some toilet paper and gave it to her. She wiped herself off. When she got up, I asked her to wait one minute, then got some additional toilet paper and wiped the back of her thighs because they were wet. Once this was done, I helped her with her undergarments.

As I was helping her, I noticed she still had the toilet paper in her hand. She then stretched her hand out and said, "What do I do with this?"

"Just put it in the toilet bowl," I said, pointing to the bowl. I guess I was a lot more tired than I thought. She turned and stuck her hand into the toilet bowl. Her hand hit the dirty water with a splashing sound and she released the toilet paper. In a loud voice I said, "No!"

Poor thing! She looked at me and said, "You told me to put it there."

I grabbed her by the hand and held her hand out. I told her, "I am sorry. Let's go wash your hands." We walked to the sink. I put some soap into her hands and made her wash and rewash her hands. I finally flushed the toilet, and then back to the room we went.

We waited another twenty-five minutes before the doctor came in. He had nothing new to tell me. He was not sure why she'd had the episode; he was not even sure what it was. Her CT scan showed nothing except what we all knew; she had issues with her brain. There was no bleeding they could see, so that ruled out a stroke. As far as he was concerned, she was okay.

We waited another fifteen minutes or so before he gave us the discharge paperwork and we left the hospital, not knowing what had caused the episode and with no information on how to handle the situation if it came up again.

When it comes to Mom's health, we are always told by doctors she is in good health except for her head. We all know that, but it would be nice to know what is going on in her head.

On the way home, I began to think about the word "hope." I used to be so hopeful for the things she could do when she got older and all the things I had hoped to do for her. Many years ago, when she was well, she had gone on a mission trip with her church from California. They went to Fiji to help build a medical center. While there she also visited New Zealand. She had such a great time! After the trip, she told me one of the local ministers did not have a pair of sneakers, so she took her sneakers and gave them to him.

Hope is defined as "the feeling that what is wanted can be had or the events will turn out for the best." This definition fills me with sadness. I wanted so much for her, but, alas, none of that will come to pass.

I asked Stephen yesterday whether he thinks hope and faith are the same. He said no, but I think they are. The Bible defines faith as "the assurance of things hoped for, the conviction of things not seen." It means we trust in something we cannot prove and will never see.

219

Before Mom got sick, I always said it is easy to have faith when things are going well, but when things go wrong, that is when faith is really tested.

I confess that since Mom got ill, I am no longer hopeful and my faith has been shattered into tiny pieces. Truthfully, I see no point in trying to pick up the pieces because I am failing whatever test this might be. If there truly is a God and this is a test to strengthen my faith, then my grade for this test would be an F. Desperation has set in and, as the Apostle Paul said, "I am a human being most miserable."

MY MAJOR MELTDOWN

Summer! What a season! I hate the summer. I am a winter person. I was born in the winter, so I'm assuming that is one of the reasons I do not like the warm weather.

It's summer 2015. Mom continues to morph into God knows what; she is medicated with at least eight pills per day. Several of them are administered in the morning to keep her calm and take away her violent behavior, and some are given at night to relax her. Most days her behavior is kept in check, but once in a while the old ghost of violence rears its ugly head.

How can she be so awful? After all these years I still can't figure this out. It hurts my heart when she behaves badly. How can one switch from being so nice for so many years to this person who, if given the chance, would rip your eyes out of your head?

One of the side effects of her medication is that it makes her very constipated. I consulted the doctor to see if there was a prescription we could give her, but it was suggested we try things on our own. In the past few months we have started buying over-the-counter medication to assist her with her bowel movements. One learns very quickly how to adjust and readjust medication to give someone in Mom's position the semblance of a life.

Once, a friend told me that most hard-core drug users don't die from overdoses because they learn what their bodies can tolerate. I now see what she meant by this because Ms. Muffin and I have learned quite well what to do for Mom when circumstances do not give the desired outcome. While the people around her tinker with her existence, Mom does not have a care in the world.

When I initially got the constipation medication, I told Ms. Muffin how much to give Mom, just to see how her body would react to the stool softener. "Only at night" was my instruction. At first it did not work well, but we kept adjusting the dose when it still did not work. I asked Ms. Muffin to increase the portion just a little; however, there was a little miscommunication and a little too much was given to Mom one particular Friday night.

Mom and I went to church on Saturday morning. At around 11:00 I asked if she needed to go the bathroom. She responded, "No." At 1:40, just before we left church, I told her I had to go to the bathroom and needed her assistance. "Go ahead without me," she said. I insisted I needed her help and finally talked her into going with me.

Once we were in the bathroom, I asked her if she had to go. "No," she repeated. I told her I wanted to pee, and once I was done she needed to pee because we had at least a half-hour drive to get to my house. Again I got the same answer: "I don't have to pee."

"Please try," I said. She finally tried and she did have to pee. Once we were finished we headed out, we got into the car for the drive home.

At home, once she was finished with her lunch, she got up and began walking around the house. I received a phone call and began a conversation. As soon as I began to talk, Mom headed up the stairs to the bathroom. My twentysomething-year-old niece had dropped by earlier; since I could not hang up the phone, I asked her to please go after Mom to be sure everything went well in the bathroom.

Less than a minute later, my niece came back and told me the bathroom door was closed. I got off the phone, went upstairs, and knocked on the door. I told Mom I was coming in. When I entered the bathroom, it was a mess, Mom was sitting on the toilet, her diaper pulled down a little past her knee, and it was full of shit. Shit was everywhere—on the toilet seat, in front of the toilet, on her hands, on the toilet paper, on the floor.

I walked over to her and said, "Honey, we have to take your boots and pants off."

She began to protest, "No, no, no, I have to do something."

I told her to give me just a moment so I could take her clothes off. As I got closer to her, she began to shift on the toilet seat. "Please, B, let me help you." Without waiting, I began taking her boots and socks off. She had diarrhea. I assumed she had begun going before she sat down on the toilet. The shit had run down her legs and had gotten on her socks and into her boots.

Once I was done taking her boots and socks off, I noticed she had a paper towel in her hand, which she had used to try to clean up some of the mess. She was about to put the paper towel in between her legs into the toilet bowl. "Please give me the paper towel because it cannot be flushed," I said. She refused to hand it over. I grabbed her hand and tried to take it from her, but she closed her hand around the paper towel. I began to apply force to her hand to get it out. I struggled with her since she was still sitting on the toilet seat. Finally, I got it out of her hand and tossed it in the direction of the boots and socks. I quickly pulled down her pants and diaper. The diaper spread even more shit, and it cascaded down her legs and thighs. I lifted her feet and out came the pants and diaper. I quickly deposited the diaper in the garbage can and then refocused my attention on Mom. I began rolling toilet paper like a madwoman and kept handing it to her, but the more I handed her, the more mess I saw. She was wiping from the front, from the back, in all directions, and the mess just kept getting worse.

Finally, when I realized we were getting nowhere, I said "B, let me give you a shower." I extended my hand to her and she shrugged. I finally stood in front of her and said, "You have to get up and get off the toilet seat."

She got up without a fuss, but when I tried to move her toward the bathtub, she stopped and said, "I took a bath already, and I am not taking another one."

I tried reasoning with her, telling her she was a mess and needed to be cleaned up. She was having none of it. When I saw she was not listening to me, I called Stephen and asked him if he could tell her through the locked door that she needed to take a bath. He did, but she still refused.

By this time she was standing close to the door with her back against the wall, half naked with her dirty butt and legs against the wall. I took a washcloth out of the shower, wet it, and tried to clean her butt. When I tried to clean her up, she turned around and yelled, "Don't touch me!"

Stephen was still standing at the door trying to reason with her and getting nowhere. He finally called my niece and asked her to come into the bathroom with me. I was crying hysterically, telling Mom I was only trying to help her. She just kept glaring at me. I got a second washcloth, soaped it, and handed it to her. She refused to take it. I tried wiping her butt again, but as soon as I tried to wipe her, she turned away and tried to open the bathroom door to leave.

I screamed at her, "You are half naked and will not go through that door!"

She screamed back, "I don't care! I am leaving anyway!"

I quickly moved to the door and held on to the knob; there we were, both of us trying as hard as we could to hold on to the doorknob. She was trying to turn it to get out; I was trying to keep it from turning to keep her in. I refused to let her out. When she realized she could not get out, she turned around and headed back to the toilet, and the shit went along with her. Every step she took left an imprint on the floor.

My niece knocked on the door; I opened it and let her in. She began trying to reason with Mom. For an instant, she seemed to listen. I then handed my niece the washcloth and told her to give it to Mom. Mom took it from her, and my niece instructed her to wipe her butt off. She complied, but as soon as she wiped her butt, she also began wiping other parts of her body, causing the shit to move to other places that were previously clean.

"B, please do not do that, you are moving the crap all over now!" I exclaimed. As soon as I said that, she came after me. Still crying, I screamed at her, "Stop! You are not going to hit me!" I guess my loud voice startled her because she took a couple of steps back and leaned against the wall. I told my niece to keep an eye on Mom.

I left the bathroom and went into the bedroom to get a change of clothes for her. I returned with the clothes and found her standing where I had left her. My niece was still washing and rewashing the washcloth in an effort to clean Mom up. Mom was still a mess. Once again I asked her to get into the tub, but the answer was the same as before—no. I got the second washcloth and kept washing it out and handing it to my niece, who in turn gave it to Mom. She was a little cleaner than when I had first entered the bathroom twenty minutes prior. However, cleaner did not mean clean. I handed Mom's clothes to my niece, and she got her to put on the clean clothes. She was finally dressed. However, there was still shit on her legs and butt. My niece got Mom to wash her hands, and I asked her to take Mom downstairs with instructions that she was not to sit on any of the living room chairs. She could sit at the table in the kitchen, but that was about it. I then tried to clean the bathroom up.

It took about twenty minutes to clean the bathroom. I flushed the toilet several times to get rid of all the stuff that was in it. I had to wash the walls, the floor, the sink, outside of the tub, and the door. I just kept washing because the smell was not leaving the room. I assumed that somehow the smell was in my brain and refused to leave, because no matter where I went in the house, even after I cleaned up the bathroom, the smell was there.

Stephen and I took Mom home once I was finished in the bathroom. On the drive, I was still crying. I could not stop; it seemed as though the stress of all the years just overwhelmed me and I could no longer control my emotions. I was a wreck.

As soon as I got Mom home, I told Ms. Muffin what had happened. She took Mom by the hand and told her she was going to take her for a bath, and off they went to the bathroom. Mom calmly walked with her, and up the stairs they went. In less than a minute, I heard the shower turn on and knew she was taking a shower.

The entire incident left me feeling so disgusted. I did not stay long at Mom's house that day. We left and returned home; once we got back I went to the bathroom and began cleaning again. I cleaned the bathroom three times on Saturday and twice again on Sunday. The smell of the shit lingered in the bathroom for an entire week.

225

Without even trying, Ms. Muffin had gotten Mom to take a shower, yet no matter what I said or did, she refused to take a shower for me.

That day in the bathroom, if Mom had struck me, I would have hit her back. This was the second time since she got sick that I thought I could hit her.

My God, why does she have to be this stubborn? I just don't get it.

THE LEANING TOWER OF PISA

It is now the end of October 2015. On the last Friday of the month, I got a call from the nurse at Mom's day care. She wanted me to know that something strange was happening with Mom. The staff noticed she was leaning to the left and was unable to sit up straight in her chair. They tried to straighten her up, but that bothered her and she pushed them away, so they were unable to make her move. She asked if Mom had fallen recently. I told her no. The nurse recommended that I take Mom to see a doctor as soon as possible. I promised her I would do it the next day.

Prior to the nurse's call, Ms. Muffin had called me to say she had observed two strange behaviors with Mom in the last couple of days. The first one was earlier in the week when they picked Mom up from day care. She was walking funny. While walking, she had her head held way back; her chest was pushed out and her back was curved. All I could think of when this was described to me was a professional ballroom dancer. In some of the dances, the woman has to hold her head all the way back while dancing. That had never seemed to be a comfortable position to hold one's body, but Mom kept that posture until she went to bed that night. When she awoke the following morning, she was leaning to the left. I did not think anything of it because with Mom we never know what is going on, and even if something is going on, by the time I get her to the doctor or hospital, whatever it is, or was, does not show up so and I just dismiss it as another thing that has no logical explanation.

As soon as I got off the phone, I called Mom's doctor. I told a nurse why I was calling and asked if Mom could be seen on Saturday, but the doctor had no Saturday hours and the next appointment was over a week away. Whatever was going on with Mom, we had to find out sooner rather than later. The nurse was kind enough to look at other offices to see if any other doctor had availability. Unfortunately, no one was seeing patients that Saturday. She then suggested I take Mom to their urgent care.

Saturday morning, I picked Mom up, and instead of heading to church we headed to the urgent care facility. It is always so stressful for me when I have to take Mom to the emergency room or to a doctor she has never seen before, because I always have to explain to each and every person who comes in contact with her what is going on.

After driving twenty minutes we arrived at the urgent care. We walked in and I explained to the receptionist why we were there. Mom was checked in, and about ten minutes later we were taken down a hall and Mom was placed on a bed. A huge curtain was drawn around her. We were instructed to take her clothes off and put a robe on her.

Here we go again was my first thought. When I told her what we needed to do, she refused to do it. I stood there with the robe in my hand and Mom on the bed. The aide who had taken us down the hall came back to do something with Mom and wanted to know why she was not changed. When I told her Mom had refused, she said, "You need to get into this robe."

Mom responded, "Sure." Only then did she allow me to take her clothes off. I slipped the robe on her and began to tie it at the back. I was about to tie the second string when the aide told me only to tie the one behind her neck because she was not sure what tests Mom would need. That was a good thing because I did not want Mom fussing with the robe.

The aide said she had to take Mom's blood pressure and temperature. I had to explain to Mom that the cuff would be a bit tight and might squeeze her arm. As soon as the cuff got tight, Mom reached for it, stating it was tight and needed to be removed. The aide said the cuff had to stay on because she needed to read her vitals. Mom kept trying to remove the cuff anyway. Once the reading was complete, the cuff came off.

The aide then tried to take Mom's temperature. Mom just looked at her. She held the device in her hand expecting Mom to comply, but that did not happen. I had previously explained to her that Mom has Alzheimer's and did not remember anything. I guess at this point the aide remembered and told Mom, "Open your mouth." Mom did. "This has to go under your tongue." No response. "Lift your tongue." Success! Her tongue was lifted and the little silver device was slipped under her tongue. "Now close your mouth." Mom did and the little device sounded an alarm; the test was done and all was well in the world again.

The aide left and told me the nurse would be in shortly. About ten minutes later the nurse came in with a chart, pen, and paper in hand. As she walked in, she moved the curtain slightly and said, "Barbara?"

Mom answered. "That's me."

The nurse said, "What brings you here today?" No response from Mom. She phrased the question a little differently: "What can we do for you today?" Still no response.

When I find myself in situations like this, I feel so helpless; I was on the verge of tears. There was Mom, lying down in the little bed, bars up on both sides. Even in the bed you could see she was leaning to the left and had no idea why she was there.

When I was much younger, cartoons on TV were not as advanced as they are today. I remember one cartoon with a character who was a little girl. She had the roundest head ever, and whenever she was upset and cried, her mouth would open up so round and the tears would just fly out from the corner of her eyes. Whenever Mom gets ill, or I assume she is ill, and I take her to the doctor or the hospital, I feel like that little girl in the cartoon. I want to open up my mouth as round as it will go and bawl my head off, and have my tears just spout out from the corners of my eyes. Of course, I am not a cartoon character and I cannot bawl and cry in public, because people would think I have lost my mind.

So instead of doing what I wanted to do, I swallowed hard and kept telling myself, *Do not cry when you speak to the nurse.*

I told the nurse Mom has Alzheimer's and was not aware of what was going on. I explained what had happened the past few days, and that was the reason we were there. She jotted down everything I said, then turned to face Mom. "Are you in pain?" Again no response.

At this point I really wanted to say to her, "You stupid cow! I just got through explaining to you Mom does not know anything. You did not listen to anything I told you." But social graces beg that I be nice, so once again I reminded her Mom was ill and had no idea what was going on. Therefore, we believed she did not know, or her brain did not tell her, when something was wrong.

"I see," the nurse said. At times I believe that most people working in the medical community have become so immune to all the illness they see that they really do not listen to anything anyone has to say. Here I was on the verge of breaking down because I had to explain in great detail what was going on with Mom and this woman was not hearing anything I said. She wrote something down and turned to leave, stating that the doctor would be in shortly. As quickly as she came, she was gone; I just stood there looking at Mom.

To my surprise, less than two minutes elapsed and she was back. "Did you fall?" she asked Mom. "Because if you did, perhaps that is the reason you are favoring your left side." I decided it was pointless to say anything to her again, because if I did, I was going to say something that I would regret. So, I said nothing. The nurse walked closer to the bed and started squeezing Mom's left hand, then slowly worked her way down her left side, squeezing as she went down. Mom did not move or make a sound. When she was finished with her squeezing, she said, "It does not seem like anything is broken." She once again turned and left the room, leaving me standing exactly where she had left me the first time.

Eventually the doctor came in. For the third time I explained what was wrong with Mom. He listened; then he went into all of his medical terminology and what he thought might be going on with her. He suggested we get a CT scan to see if there was anything new going on in her head. I agreed and he left. We waited and waited for the technician to come, for more than an hour. The doctor kept coming by; each time he asked if the tech had come by, and each time I had the same answer—no. He apologized and said because it was Saturday, things were a little slower since they were not fully staffed. By now, thankfully, Mom had nodded off and I did not have to worry about her trying to escape from the bed.

Finally, the tech arrived and Mom was placed in a wheelchair to go for the test. I was allowed to accompany her. On the long walk to the scanning room, I again had to explain that Mom has Alzheimer's and would need to be restrained once she was placed in the machine. The tech told me they had no restraints, but he would do his best. Once we arrived at the designated scanning room, he asked me to accompany him into the room. He was the only person working, so while he spoke to Mom, explaining what was going to take place, I kept telling Mom she would be okay and to listen to the nice man. It took him several minutes to get her onto the small bedlike structure; then he walked over, got some purple tape, and taped Mom's head down. It was an open scan machine with a huge round section for the head area. Once he was finished he instructed Mom not to move, then pressed a button on the machine and the bedlike portion moved her head area into the big round section of the machine. He kept telling her not to move because he was going to take a picture of her head. She said that her head was too tight and started trying to take the tape off. By this time, we were both in the second room with the equipment and computers. Mom started to move, so he had to return to the room not once but twice to readjust her. He then returned to the room and just kept repeating, "You have to lie still. I need to take pictures of your head." In less than three minutes, he was finished, and for the first time since Mom had become ill I saw her brain.

It is said that knowledge is a good thing, but in this case too much knowledge is bad. The tech said he had to go through the pictures to be sure that all of them were fine. As he moved from frame to frame, the horror of it all hit me like a ton of bricks.

It was like a slow-moving slide show. From the front, I could see all the bones, the outline of her jaw, even the partial in her mouth. I saw the back of her head and the side of her head—everything was a light gray color. And then a slide showed the top of her head. The view from the top of her head was quite different from the rest of the slides. This view showed two large, very dark patches at the top of her brain, and I realized that in layman's terms she literally had a hole in her brain. The big dark spot on the top of her brain was where the plaque had eaten through her brain. I just stood there and could not believe what I was seeing. I felt a little woozy and sick to my stomach, and that sick feeling stayed with me for several days after our visit to the urgent care.

When the slide show was finished, the tech hit the button and Mom moved out from the machine. He cut the bandage off her head and the two of us helped her off the bed and back into the wheelchair. He wheeled her down the long hallway and back into the room.

Once we were back in the room, I took the robe off and put her clothes on. I told her she had to get back into the bed. I got a magazine for her because I knew she would not want to stay in bed too long. As soon as she got back into the bed, she told me she had to get out. I told her I could not move the bars on the bed. She tried putting her feet through the bars but did not get very far. When that did not work, she began moving slowly to the end of the bed. When I saw her moving down the bed, I knew I had to block her. There was a table left in the room that was used for meals. I rolled it very close to the bed and leaned on it so my weight kept it in place. By the time she got to the end of the bed, she was blocked in. I handed her the magazine and told her there were a lot of lovely baby pictures to look at, and was relieved when she took it from me and began to look through it. She kept looking at the magazine for almost forty-five minutes. Thank you, Lord, for small mercies!

The doctor came by a couple of times to let me know he was waiting for the test results, and once he got them he would come right back. Each time he came, he asked me if I was all right and I said yes.

I often wonder what anyone would do if I told them how I actually felt. How should you feel in a situation of like this? You are never all right. I know he was trying to lighten the moment, but what was I supposed to say? Of course I was not all right, but I guess it would have been a bit on the rude side if I were to say, "Well, I just saw my mom's dead brain, and truth be told, I feel like screaming my head off because the entire thing is just too much to handle." That was exactly what I was thinking, but the thought had to remain unspoken.

Finally, the doctor came in with the results. He gently touched my shoulder. "As you know, your Mom's brain is atrophying." As soon as he said the word, I thought to myself, *Hum, now there is a word—"atrophy."* For a few seconds, I thought that sounded like a French word and immediately thought, *What if we were in a French restaurant and the doctor was the waiter and he came over and said to Mom, "Madam, how would you like a side of atrophy with the meal you ordered? The atrophy is quite lovely today."*

While I was thinking these silly things, I could still hear the doctor talking, but I was not really paying attention to him. Then he said, "Well, if you want to, we can put her in the hospital for a few days and do a battery of tests to be sure everything is all right." Back to reality I snapped, and he continued, "We see no swelling, no bleeding as far as we can tell. This might be just another manifestation of her disease. The leaning to one side may go away after a few days or it may stay permanently. There is no way we can tell what will happen. But as far as we are concerned, we don't see anything out of the ordinary."

I told him I could not put her in the hospital for days because the only way to keep her in bed would be to restrain her, and I could not do that to her. He said he understood fully. He wished me luck with Mom and asked me if I needed copies of his diagnosis.

"No, thank you," I responded.

"If you need anything in the future, please do not hesitate to give me a call." He handed me his card. I thanked him and told Mom we would be leaving. I rolled the table away from the foot of the bed and helped her off. We slowly made our way down the hall and out the big door to the waiting room, and exited the building.

As we were walking down the path from the building to the parking lot, Mom looked down and saw the dirt next to the walkway. She said, "I could have some dirt for lunch today."

I said, "Today is not a dirt day. We will be going home to have a late lunch." It was now past lunchtime, and I assumed this was Mom's way of telling me she was hungry.

After we got into the car, I slowly drove through the parking lot and out onto the main road, leaving the good doctor and the building behind. I knew in my heart that from that day forward, I would know much more about Mom than I had before, because I had seen for myself what this disease had done to her brain. It literally had eaten the top part of her brain away.

LOST

My brother, Nick, has been living in Australia for the past fifteen years with his family. He has visited us twice since his move. He has been spared the pain of watching Mom slide off the deep end. I wish he was around. I adore him; he is the only brother I have. I tell him how sad it makes me that he is not here. He just walked away and left us all behind.

I know we all have our own lives to live, but it would have been extremely helpful if he lived closer to us. I saw a picture of him on Facebook a few months ago. He was surrounded by strangers (strangers to me, not him). I felt jealous because he has a new family and friends, and his own family in the United States does not seem to factor into his life at all. I wonder if I could have been that brave or selfish to walk away from everything and everyone I know and not look back.

He has carved out a life for himself separate from us and Mom, and that to me just adds to the sadness of this ugly situation. For all the years he has been away, we communicate mostly by e-mail.

It was getting close to Christmas 2015, and he told me it had been some time since he had spoken to Mom and he was going to call her on Christmas Day. I do my best not to complain to him about how terrible Mom's health is because, as far as I am concerned, it would not make a difference. I advised him not to call because she does not know who he is. What's the point?

From my perspective, his mother-in-law became his mom. When she was very ill, he and his wife took her in and cared for her until she died. For the past fifteen years, Mom has been his mother only through DNA, nothing else. He knows nothing about her daily life or the progression of her disease. After I told him not to call, he asked if she is now totally lost. I said not totally lost but almost.

Ms. Muffin left on vacation, and we have a part-time person looking after Mom for a month. The caregiver called and asked for my assistance, because she said she had negotiated with Mom all day, trying to talk her into taking a bath, and had no luck. I left work early and went over. I arrived around 4:00. Mom was resting. I walked up the stairs and gently touched her feet and called her name. "Wake up. You have to take a bath," I said.

She turned and looked at me and said, "Who are you?"

I wanted to cry as soon as she asked who I was. "It's me, B. I came to see you." Then I began to coax her out of bed. It took more than half an hour to get her showered and changed.

On the train going home the other day, there was a man sitting one seat away from me with his two young children, and whenever the little girl behaved badly, he said to her, "If you continue to behave badly, I will leave you on the train." Each time he told her he would leave her, in the smallest and saddest voice she could muster, she said, "Please don't leave me."

I feel like that little girl. Mom has now left me behind. What am I supposed to do when she asks me who I am? There is no way for my brain to process this information. I am her child. How can she not recognize me?

I see her all the time and she does not know who I am. She has not seen my brother since she got ill. There is no way she would know who he is. I am not sure whether or not he called; I never asked. It really does not matter now, because her knowledge of her children is gone forever.

THE DEARLY DEPARTED . . .
THAT DIDN'T DEPART

I have a friend whose father has Alzheimer's and is expected to die any day now. His father had a stroke and had to be placed in an assisted-living home because he became too violent for his mother to handle.

My friend and I are soldiers on the battlefield with this terrible disease—foot soldiers, so to speak, fighting a war we know we have already lost.

As the years passed, we swapped horror stories about the disease. We sometimes cry together because of the helplessness we feel. It is true—misery does love company, and trust me, this disease is pure misery.

I knew when his father stopped recognizing him that it broke his heart. He referred to the time as being lost to his father forever. He is also aware that Mom doesn't recognize me. We seem to be partners in a dance of coincidence, an ironic ballad about the "dear almost departed." Our parents are deceased in one sense but very much alive in another. Or maybe I should say they are dead enough for us to mourn but just alive enough to remind us they are not truly dead.

His father came to visit him a few weeks ago and had a second stroke. The doctors believed it was the "big one." He described in detail everything that had happened. In our situation, we relate everything down to the smallest detail. Somehow, I think it makes us feel better because we are treating our parents as if they are still alive and able to understand everything. Because we know they cannot understand, we want others to know exactly what is going on and how utterly helpless we are.

My friend's father stayed at a local hospital for a week. His right side was completely paralyzed. His father lived in New England, seven hours away, and the local hospital refused to release him unless they found a rehabilitation center close to his current nursing home. Once they found a facility, his father was driven by ambulance all the way there.

His father was doing reasonably well in rehabilitation for the first week. The second week, he had a massive stroke that left him brain-dead. He died a couple of days later.

When my friend told me his father had died, I was so happy for him. I know that sounds horrible, but this disease takes such a toll on its victims and their families that each time I hear of the death of someone with Alzheimer's, I say, "Thank God, and God bless that family."

After the death of his father, we talked about his mom and how she is coping. I am positive she is relieved her husband is no longer a stranger to himself and to her. To lighten the moment, the other day I told him I had read an article about the disease that stated the mother is the carrier of the gene for the disease. I said, "There is one less thing for you to worry about, because you will never get the disease." We both laughed an uneasy laugh because, really, no one knows for sure who will get this disease.

DANGER

The New Year came and went without much of anything—no big celebration for Christmas or New Year. What is there to celebrate? Not much, if you ask me. It is now February 2016. It has been a very warm winter, with the exception of a couple of bad snowstorms.

I picked Mom up and came back to my house. When we got back I decided it would be good to give her something to drink. I told her I was going to make some tea for her. Because I cannot keep her out of my kitchen, I put the teapot on the back burner and turned it on. I went to get something out of the fridge, and when I turned around Mom was standing at the stove with her hands outstretched. She was about to touch the teapot. I did not have time to get to her before she touched the pot, so I yelled "B, do not touch that!"

She did a double take and looked at me. "I just wanted to see if it was hot." By that time I was next to her and grabbing her hands. She pulled away from me and stormed out of the kitchen. "I was not going to do anything."

The next week, on Sunday, Mom went to Sally's house to visit. Sally had a pot of water on the stove. The phone rang and she left the kitchen to answer it. She was out of the kitchen for less than one minute. When she came back, Mom was in the process of putting her hands in the boiling water. Sally quickly got in between Mom and the stove and stood in front of Mom. Mom started to argue with her that she just wanted to see if the water was hot. Who in their right mind would want to touch a hot teapot or put her hands into boiling water? The answer—Mom!

NEVER BORROW TROUBLE

When we were kids, my maternal grandmother had an adage that went something like this: "Never borrow trouble from tomorrow because we have enough trouble today." With Mom's illness, it's so easy to borrow trouble from tomorrow.

The unknown is so scary. Science knows so little about this disease. I read an article a few days ago that claimed certain drugs may slow the progression of the disease. I have proof the claim in the article is incorrect. The medication Mom is taking for her brain has not worked, and I don't believe any medication will work, because by the time a patient or loved one realizes that something is wrong, it is too late.

Money, as they say, makes the world go around, and I believe more money is needed for research, but the article stated that this is not in anyone's budget. Therefore, the only thing that is known is that in the future more people will suffer from this disease.

There was a second article I read in the local paper about a doctor in New Jersey who was conducting a clinical trial with Alzheimer's patients. The drug he was using came from a huge pharmaceutical company. The company discovered the drug was making patients worse than they had been before they entered the study. The drug was pulled and the clinical trial stopped. The doctor said he assumed many of the families would call him to complain, but to his surprise not one person called. They all just moved on to the next trial, hoping to find something that could help. So it seems I have borrowed trouble, not only from tomorrow but from the day after, and the next day, and for as long as Mom lives. I know I would not want to live with this disease, but how would I know if I am getting it? And if I am getting it, what could I do to prevent it?

In an episode of the original *Twilight Zone* series, a man keeps appearing in random places to a woman driving alone across the country. She becomes very afraid of him. Finally, she calls home and learns that there was an accident several days prior, and she had died. She gets back in the car and sees the same man in the rearview mirror. He is sitting in the backseat and asks, "Going my way?" She realizes he is the Grim Reaper.

I suppose we all are unwilling participants who have, through no fault of our own, borrowed too much trouble from the never-ending tomorrows, and the Grim Reaper is our constant companion, always following us around wanting to know if we are going his way!

REDEMPTION

The Bible teaches that our first parents were perfect, but in order to keep their perfect state they had to pass a test. Unfortunately for us, they failed and fell from grace. But there was a provision in God's contract that held out the hope of redemption. This hope was provided in order to give our first parents and their offspring a way to be restored to their original perfect state.

What does redemption mean, anyway? Based on my understanding of the word, it means to restore or give back something that was desirable and was lost, not forever but for a while. From this perspective, I am seeking redemption for Mom, redemption from the disease. I seek a restoration of who and what she was—a give-back of her mind, so to speak. I don't think that is too much to ask of a God who claims to be good and kind, a God who holds our very existence in His hands. I want and seek redemption, as per His promise, for the one I love. I pray for this to happen, even if that restoration comes from human hands. If God is unwilling or unable to give Mom His redemption, then He is capable of making it happen another way. I pray that He will give someone somewhere—in a laboratory, a hospital, or in a research center, wherever it may be—the knowledge to unlock and somehow reverse the effects of this disease and give Mom redemption along with millions of others suffering from this affliction.

The Bible is full of doom and destruction. In many places it talks about the destruction that occurred when swarms of locusts came to town. They ate everything in sight, and when they left there was nothing. I view this disease like the locusts of old; Alzheimer's leaves nothing behind.

I prayed to God: "If You are listening, may You have mercy and allow redemption to come quickly to Mom."

THE MERRY-GO-ROUND

I've always been an animal lover. I've always had pets: dogs, lots of cats, birds, goats, fish, chickens—you name it, I've had it. A few years ago, I owned three cats: Degas, Van Gogh, and Eli.

Van Gogh died first, after sixteen and a half years. I came home from work one night and found him sitting on his chair in the basement. When I called him he refused to move, which was odd. Finally, I went over to the chair, picked him up, and put him down on the floor. Once he was on the floor, he refused to put his front paw down. I took him to the vet that night and they tried to convince me he had gotten his paw caught in something in the house and it was broken. I had a cat-proof house; there was no way he had gotten his paw caught in anything. We had to leave him overnight. The following day his leg was scanned. He had cancer. The tumor was so large that it had pushed his front leg out of the socket. The doctor wanted to amputate his leg and give him chemotherapy. I told the doctor he had been such a good friend and I would not put him through that kind of pain. We decided to put him to sleep.

Degas lived another year and a half. He used to be my fat cat, weighing in at a hefty sixteen pounds. By the time I put him to rest, he was only seven pounds. He kept losing weight. When he began to look like a ghost, at seventeen and a half years old, I knew it was time to let him go.

They both had a wonderful life and brought lots of laughter and happiness to our lives. I still miss them. Eli was put down three years after Degas. He too was a fat guy. When I took him in as an adult, he weighed twenty-seven pounds. The lady who gave him to me weighed approximately ninety-five pounds. I think because she did not eat, she fed him more food than he needed. He too had grown on us and was a good companion. I am not sure if he ever truly loved us, but it does not matter, because we loved him.

The one pet I've always wanted and could never afford was a horse. They are such majestic creatures. Having a horse is an expensive endeavor, and Mom could never afford one. Because owning a horse was out of the question, I transferred my affection from the horse to the carousel. In my opinion, carousels are beautiful. Even if they are located in the cheapest amusement park, I still see the beauty in them—horses that go up and down and around in a circle. Someone can get on and off without incurring the high costs of owning a horse. With the music and the people, especially the children, everyone always seems so happy on a carousel.

When Mom was well, she always referred to carousels as merry-go-rounds, and that is exactly what her life has become, but no one is merry on this ride. The music and the horses never stop. Everything just keeps going round and round, and no matter how tired or bored we get, this ride will not end well.

Mom's disease has cast such a long, dark shadow on my life. At times I feel like I am in the deep end of the pool and the water is just under my nostrils. If I breathe too deeply, the water will overtake me and I will go under, never to rise again. Most times it is so overwhelming, I think I forget to breathe. The sad part about this whole thing is there is no way to escape it. All the "ifs" in the world cannot change what is going on, and no matter what I do, it will not get better. The days pass and nothing good happens. The disease marches on at its own pace, doing exactly what it wants to do and we all are just along for the ride.

I was reading an article a few weeks ago regarding caregivers who provide care for their loved ones who have this disease. According to the article, some people are in the beginning stages of the disease while others have had the disease for years. One man who had just been diagnosed with the disease stated he and his wife were looking to move to one of the few states where euthanasia is legal. He said he did not want to burden his wife with his care when he gets sicker and cannot remember anything.

The article also talked about a support group for caregivers. One of the caregivers whose wife is sick said he asked how many of the group members were on anti-depressants, and almost half the hands in the room went up. He said he himself is now on antidepressants and he believes that the majority of people in the room were taking something for depression.

Each day I feel like there is a huge black cloud that follows me around; no matter where I go, I can feel it with me. I don't know if this is a symptom of depression. This invisible cloud is there day and night; no matter what I do, no matter where I go, I am unable to shake it. Once someone told me there are no "shadows in darkness." This is not true because even in darkness I see the shadow of that dark cloud.

I don't want Mom to live like this, but I know she could live this way for another ten to fifteen years. The other day I mentioned to Ms. Muffin we have to be careful and take care of ourselves by not worrying too much because we all could die and leave Mom behind, and that would be the greatest tragedy of all.

Melodrama has never been my style. But my God, how much can one person take? Who knows what is in store for any of us?

A few months ago, Amy came to visit us. Poor thing—she is still struggling with her memory issues from her stroke. She said she is afraid she may become like Mom. What kind of response do you give someone when he or she says something like this? Some scientists believe if you keep active, you can delay the full onset of the disease. Is this true? I don't know. I don't think anyone knows.

A few nights ago, Sally called me crying hysterically. I could not understand what she was saying. I thought something awful had happened. I kept saying, "What is wrong?" She kept crying. Finally, after a few minutes, she calmed down enough to tell me she was doing something with her daughter and she had forgotten a word, a common everyday word she just could not remember, so she was freaking out.

For individuals whose families are not plagued with this disease, a situation like this would bring a different response. Maybe they would not even think twice about the entire thing. However, when you have a mother or a father with Alzheimer's, the first thing you think is, *My God! Am I getting Alzheimer's?* This is not the type of life anyone should have to live. Fear is a terrible, uneasy roommate, and for the family of someone with this disease it's a roommate that you see each time you look at that person. When you look in the mirror, you wonder what is lurking behind your eyes—or worse, you wonder what is going on in your brain that is hidden away. You keep wondering, *Will my turn come to get this disease?*

My wish is to wake up one day and know this was just a bad dream, but I know this is reality and day by day we will have to learn how to fool ourselves into not always freaking out when we fail to remember a word or a name.

And so the merry-go-round keeps going up and down and round and round, and we all became captive participants without an escape in this horrible game.

TIME

In November of 2016 I had to move Mom from the day care she had attended for years. She had become too much for the workers to handle. First they cut her hours. We were asked to bring her later in the morning and pick her up before the end of the program. Several weeks later, Ms. Muffin was told to come to the center around noon and sit with Mom until she had to go home. I knew it was time to move her. I found another day care closer to her home. I thought it was a much better arrangement because they would pick her up and drop her off each day.

The first week at the day care went well, but by the second week she did not want to get off the van at the end of the day. It took an average of five to fifteen minutes to get her off. The center catered to other clients who were mentally challenged, and at the end of the day when Mom refused to get off the van, the clients on the van got very upset and began to cry, and some even bit themselves.

A cousin suggested that if we gave Mom a doll, that would keep her calm and perhaps get her off the van without further problems. We got the doll, but that only worked for a week or two.

In January 2017, she had her first accident at the new day care. She pooped on herself. She allowed the workers to clean her up, and we picked her up half an hour after the incident.

In March she had a second incident, but this time she did not allow anyone to touch her. She walked all over the center and created a huge mess. The nurse called my office, but I was in a meeting and did not listen to the message until an hour later. By the time I called, the damage was done.

The following day, I spoke to the director of the program and he informed me he had to have the center professionally cleaned; it cost over two hundred dollars for the cleaning. I had to pay the bill.

He also let me know that Mom was declining and they had done all they could for her. He wished me good luck. That was the last day she went to day care.

Since that incident, Mom has stopped going to the bathroom. I am not sure why this is going on. Currently she is pooping only a couple times per week, and when she does, she just goes wherever she is.

I took her to the doctor. They prescribed a stool softener for her, but that is not working. She has finally become incontinent.

WHY ME?

I often say to my family jokingly that if I were married to anyone other than my husband, by now I would be divorced. Stephen is the kindest, most generous person I have ever known, and I am not saying this just because he is my husband. Prior to marrying him we were friends, and we are still best friends. Before I married him, I told him how important my family is to me, and he has stood by me no matter what I have to do.

He and I have full financial responsibility for Mom. I spend so much money on her. When she first began behaving badly, I did not know exactly what to do but knew I needed help, so I called the local hospital and asked to speak to a social worker. Once I told the social worker my story, she said, "Your mother is not your responsibility. Bring her to the hospital, drop her off, and tell the receptionist you can no longer take care of her. She will be turned over to the state. They will find some place to put her, and once she is settled you will receive a call telling you where she is."

I was shocked. "It's my mom you are talking about. I cannot do that."

"Yes, you can. She is not your responsibility."

I hung up, and of course I did not drop her off at the hospital. How could I do that? I would not drop my pets off and give up responsibility for them; they are animals and I could never do that. I couldn't imagine dropping Mom off and washing my hands of her. I would die of guilt.

We don't want to put Mom in a nursing home. The financial burden is huge, but we keep plugging along.

Initially when I asked Sally to assist us financially, she told me her children will put her in a home if something ever happens to her. As soon as she said that, I knew what it meant.

It is our choice to care for Mom, and we are on our own. I can't bring myself to think about Mom in a nursing home. If I put her there, she will be dead in a few months. I am sure of that.

I know it is unfair that Stephen and I have to take care of her, but this is the choice that we think was made for us and we are just along for the ride. Does it bother me that we are the only ones taking care of her? Of course it does, but I cannot abandon her just because we do not have help. She is my mom; she dedicated most of her life to taking care of us, and now in her hour of need I do not have it in me to turn my back on her. It's like that line in the Billy Joel song "I've Loved These Days" about the money coming and going. The only difference here is that I don't love these days.

Last year I got a small bonus. I told Stephen I was going to take the money and spend it on myself. I have never done this before, but since we have to spend a lot of our money on Mom, I decided it was time to splurge and do something for me. I went to our local jeweler and chose two rings. I paid for one in cash and put the second one on my credit card. I felt really good that for once I had done something for me.

We should be able to live the way we want to, but we don't. I was hoping I could retire in in my fifties; I can't. If Mom is still alive ten years from now, I will be in my sixties and still working to support her. This is not fair to us, but that is how life has turned out. I could continue to ask "Why us?", but that would not change anything.

We have made a commitment to her, and we intend to keep it until Mom is no more!

A CHAIR IS STILL A CHAIR

At the end of 2016 I stopped taking Mom to church. This chapter of her life, like so many others, is now closed forever.

After church I went to visit her. Sally came later, and when she walked in she said to Mom, "May I kiss you?" In the past, the answer to this question had always been no. However, today the answer was yes. Sally kissed her and asked for a second kiss; the answer again was yes.

Well, you could have knocked me over with a feather. Sally just kept kissing Mom. She then asked if she could sit in Mom's lap; again the answer was yes. She sat down, and a few seconds later Mom said, "Too heavy." Sally moved and sat next to Mom, leaning on her for the longest time.

It had been over a decade since Mom allowed Sally to get close to her. All the hatred and mistrust of Sally had finally drained out of her head.

When Mom forgot who I was, she still remembered Sally. We thought she would never forget her, but the day finally came and that memory is gone. It would be nice to say it is a good thing she has forgotten Sally, but it is not. The reason? It means she has sunk closer to her demise.

In Mom's house we have a brown loveseat in the living room. A few weeks after she allowed Sally to hug and kiss her, she walked over to the loveseat and began shaking it. She kept saying, "Sally, Sally!" When the loveseat did not respond, Mom walked over to Sally's old bedroom door and turned the knob, but the door was locked. She kept turning the knob and tried so hard to get the door open. Mom saw her reflection in the glass pane of the door and in a low voice she said, "Let me . . ." She could not finish the sentence. She had no idea it was just her reflection she was seeing. When she could not get into the room, she simply walked away.

THE NOISE

At 6:00 on March 31, 2017, I was getting ready for work when the phone rang. When the phone rings early in the morning or late at night, I always know it is not good news. It was Sally. She sounded out of breath. She said, "It's Mom," and told me to speak to Ms. Muffin. She came on and said Mom was breathing strangely, and she had tried for more than five minutes to wake her up and she was unresponsive. I told her to call 911 and I would come over as soon as I could.

Once the ambulance arrived, Sally and Cindy followed it to the hospital, and Ms. Muffin waited for me. I took a quick shower and headed out. I picked Ms. Muffin up at 7:15. On our way to the hospital, Ms. Muffin told me she had woken up with the impression that there was some kind of roadwork being done in front of the house. She thought it was a bit early for the town to be scraping the street, so she looked through the window but saw no one. She then realized the sound was not coming from outside but from Mom's room. She went into the room and Mom was making a funny sound. When she tried to wake Mom, she did not respond. Ms. Muffin tried for five minutes, then called Sally and Cindy. They came over and also tried in vain to get Mom up.

The ambulance took about five minutes to arrive, and when the paramedics arrived Mom was still unresponsive. It took over fifteen minutes for Mom to come out of whatever was going on with her.

It took Ms. Muffin and me about twenty minutes to get to the hospital. When we arrived we were directed to Mom's room. Sally and Cindy were sitting in the room and Mom was asleep. Sally said the doctor had already ordered a brain scan for Mom and they had just brought her back to the room.

A few minutes later, one of the emergency room doctors came into the room with his hand outstretched. He greeted us with, *"Buenos dias, señoras. Como estan todos? ¿Qué te trajo hoy a nuestro hospitál?"*

I could not believe he would enter a room like this. Mom's last name is Spanish, so he assumed we did not speak English. Sally rose from her chair and said, "She speaks English."

"Oh, sorry. I was just practicing my Spanish." I thought how stupid some people could be at times. He proceeded to let us know that the first test they took was inconclusive. Perhaps she had a mini stroke, but it was not showing up on the test. According to him, at times the results to confirm a stroke do not show up immediately.

He went on to give us a long list of tests that he wanted to perform. One test involved injecting dye into Mom to see her arteries. I immediately objected. I told him she would not stay still for this test to be performed and I would not give permission for him to do it.

He said okay and left the room. About forty-five minutes later a worker came in and said they were taking Mom for some additional testing. She began pushing the bed out of the room. As soon as she exited the room, she said to one of the nurses at the nurses' station, "This one does not speak English."

I was walking behind her and said, "She speaks English. Because of her disease she does not understand what is being said."

We moved farther down the hallway and the aide saw another attendant coming toward her. She said to her, "You speak Spanish, don't you?" The young lady said she did. "Well, this one does not speak English and I need a translator." Again I told her Mom spoke English. Going to the hospital with Mom really stinks; no one ever listens to anything I have to say. I wasn't speaking in a whisper or anything like that; they simply did not listen.

We got to the testing room and the nurse told us to wait outside. They took Mom into the room. Less than three minutes later, the door opened and the nurse wheeled Mom out. They said they could not do the test because Mom would not lie still and they could not inject her with the dye.

"The dye?" I asked. "There must be a mistake because I specifically told the doctor not to order that test."

The nurse saw I was upset. "I will have the doctor come back and speak to you, but for now the test has to be placed on hold."

Mom was taken back to the room. About half an hour later the doctor came back. He said he was told I did not want Mom to take one of the tests he had ordered. I was now beyond annoyed and said to him, "You did not listen to anything I told you. When we spoke before, I specifically told you Mom would not stay still for the test and you went ahead and ordered it anyway."

He said, "I am the emergency room doctor and I am trying to figure out what is wrong with her. You don't want certain things done, but I am doing what is best for the patient and I am a trained professional."

Before he could continue, I cut him off. "I am not questioning your education or professionalism. I am just telling you as someone who has cared for her for the past seven years, I know what she will allow you to do and what cannot be done. However, you decided to do what you wanted to do, and what I told you would happen just happened and the test was not done."

"In that case," he said, "we will run the other tests, but you will have to leave her in the hospital for observation."

I said the only way she would be able to stay in the hospital was if she was restrained, because once she was feeling better, she would not stay in the bed.

"That is inhumane and we don't do that in this hospital," the doctor said.

"I am telling you what will happen, and for your information, I will not be leaving her here overnight." At this point, I could tell he was annoyed. He just turned and left the room.

I texted Stephen and told him what happened. Stephen called me later and told me the doctor would not come back to the room. He was correct. We stayed in the hospital for another six hours and the doctor never returned. Several other tests were done, and at around 6:00 p.m. another doctor came in to chat with us. He said they wanted to keep Mom and continue testing to see if anything showed up on her brain. I repeated what I had told the first doctor, that I would not leave her. He told me it was my choice and he left.

At 6:30, after having been in the hospital for almost eleven hours, I went out to the nurses' station and asked if the test results were in. They were in, so I asked for the results. The nurse said she would come to the room in a few minutes to have a discussion with me.

She came in five minutes later and said they had found nothing wrong and they were going to admit Mom. I repeated that she would not be staying. The nurse said I would have to sign a form that I was taking her without the doctor's consent. I was concerned that if I signed the form and something happened, they would not admit her if I had to bring her back. The nurse assured me they would admit her if that occurred. Once she said this, I signed the paperwork. Once it was signed, we got Mom dressed and left the hospital.

Mom was still a bit out of it, but I knew it would be better for her to be at home instead of the hospital. We never found out what was wrong with her.

THE VALUE OF A LIFE

When I was in graduate school, I had to take a statistics class. One of the projects we had to complete required us to figure out the value of someone's life. It was basic stuff. You evaluated the person's education level, their age, and where they lived. Based on their education, you calculated their earning power and cross-indexed it with how many years they lived. Naturally, different people had different life values in comparison to others. If someone had an advanced degree and lived in a certain part of town, his or her life would be worth more than that of the guy who lived in a bad neighborhood with a high school education. Nothing personal—that is just the way it works.

If I were to run the same scenario on Mom and apply it to her life, her life would mirror that of the person in the bad neighborhood who had a high school education. On second thought, her life might be worth even less. She never finished grade school, much less high school. She never had good jobs and never earned a lot of money; she came from the wrong side of the tracks. From a statistical point of view, her life is not worth much, but from my perspective her life is worth so much more than money.

Mom's worth has always been beyond measure. Were it possible, I would do anything to restore her to what made her my beautiful mom. But that dice, alas, is not mine to roll; it was cast a long time ago, way before anyone, including Mom, realized it. The dice is now slowly rolling and will eventually come to a stop. When will it stop? I do not know. The only thing I am sure of is that she will never get better and with each passing day she will become sicker, so I wait for the inevitable, all the while knowing that the worst part of this disease is yet to come.

ABOUT THE AUTHOR

S. P. Murray grew up in Crown Heights, Brooklyn, with her mom (Barbara) and three siblings. She has the soul of an artist but makes a living working in the banking industry. She is a certified nutritionist (herbal medicine), holds BA and MS degrees, and believes that, in spite of what we see, mankind can still be good, kind, and brave.

She is a dreamer who comes up with fanciful ideas that may never come to pass, but that does not stop her from dreaming. Her belief is that "you must build the castles in the air before you can move them down to earth." She believes with all her heart that dreams are what make us who we are, and some dreams can come true.

She has been married to her husband, S. P. Murray, for twenty-three years and lives in New Jersey. She loves animals, and she and her husband are kept by their two cats, Phoenix and Hope.

Review Requested:
If you loved this book, would you please provide a
review at Amazon.com?